M OVIE IND

Directing the Theater of Your Mind

D1714517

L. Michael Hall, Ph.D.

Published by:
  Neuro-Semantics®
  P.O. Box 8
  Clifton, CO. 81520   USA
  (970) 523-7877

Printed By:
  Action Printing
  Jerry Kucera, Owner
  516 Fruitvale Court, Unit C
  Grand Jct. CO. 81504
  (970) 434-7701
  Actionpres@aol.com

Artwork and Cover Design by *Doug Clary*
  Action Printing
  Grand Junction, CO. 81504

ISNS: The International Society of Neuro-Semantics
Institutes of Neuro-Semantics Web Sites:

www.neurosemantics.com
www.neurosemantics.org
www.runyourownbrain.com

MovieMind

PREFACE

Hello David, what can I do for you? What's on your mind today?
I need more motivation. Sometimes I just don't seem to
be able to get myself going.

Are we talking about work, fitness, relationships or what?
Oh, work. Business. I'm sick and tired of living paycheck
to paycheck and I have plenty of opportunities to increase
my income, but when I sit down to actually do something
about it, I just don't feel motivated.

If I were to peek into the theater of your mind and see what you
are seeing, what would I see? How do you represent increasing
your income?
Hmmmm... I really don't think I have a Movie ... I just
talk to myself. I just say, "I need to get with it."

Sounds like a really boring Movie. If that's all I had going on in
my mind about becoming more successful in business, I'd be
yawning too and wanting to change channels. I'd have no
motivation either.
So what am I to do?

Well, first how about create a much more exciting and dramatic
mental Movie that you'd find compelling, "How to Become a
Success at Work."
That's just it. When you say that, I don't find that
interesting.

Hmmmm. So, why do you say you *"need* to get with it?"" When you "get with it" and do what you do, what do you get from that? How is that important for you?

> Well, I would have more money, enough money to pay my bills then.

Okay, and when you have enough money for your bills, what do you get from that?

> Well, I don't have to worry about my bills.

That sounds important. [Yes.] So, how is that important? When you move beyond worrying about bills, what do you then think about? What do you get from that which is even more important?

> I don't know. ... I guess a sense of freedom to do what I want to do.

And what's that? What do you want to do?

> Hmmmm. I suppose I'd like to work with kids in teaching team building skills. That's what I'd like to do, but I know I can't make a living doing that.

As you describe that, it sounds like that would be valuable to you. [Yeah, it would!] So, why is that important? What do you get out of that which is even more important to you?

> If I could do that I'd feel like I was doing something significant, doing something that really counts, making a difference.

So you'd like to do that?

> Yes I would!

Let's say you did. Let's say that somehow you got to do that for a living ... how would that delight and please you, above and beyond contributing and doing something significant? What would you be getting that's even more important than that?

I'd get a sense of fulfillment, like my life is fitting into a larger purpose and that would bring a higher sense of joy or happiness.

Good. That's sounds important... so just be with those thoughts and those feelings and whatever images and sights and sounds and experiences come to mind when you think about working with kids ... just let all of that turn into a Movie in your mind ... that's right ... and as you do, step into that Movie for just a moment ... so that you can begin to imagine what it would really be like to be *inside* that Movie and seeing it from the inside and as you do ... mmmmmm ... just enjoy it and let the Movie become even richer, brighter, fuller ... and do you like that? [Shaking his head yes.] And what if ... I know this is hard to believe, but what if ... this could become a future reality in a few years ... just imagine being a little older, wiser, more skilled ... imagine becoming the You inside this Movie who can do this with skill and confidence ... And you can say "Ahhhhh!" or "Mmmmmmmmmm" to feel the pleasure ... and suppose you woke up tomorrow and all of the tomorrows thereafter *with this Movie in mind* ... and began to take the necessary steps to make it real, would you like that? [Yes I would!] And would you have any problem with motivation then? [No, none.]

Well, you can't have this dream. You can't have this Movie as a vision of your future ... it's mine!
    No, it is not! It's mine.
But it doesn't fit with what you really want!
    Yes it does. It really does fit. I like it.

No, you're just saying that. You won't remember this? You won't keep these feelings in your mind or in your body.
    Ha. That's what you think. Thanks.
And so it came to pass.

M OVIE IND

Your mind is like a Movie ... on your internal Big Screen you flash snapshots of sights, images, and scenarios and you also play snippets of Movie sequences and even full-length epic features. You do it all in that private entertainment center we call "Mind." This is how we *think* and learn and even reason. Some people are more visual learners, others learn best by hearing, others learn best by doing to get a feel of things, and yet others are primarily linguistic learners.

What happens though when we close our eyes or just de-focus them and "think" about things? What Movies play out on the theater of our mind?

Horror Movies that would make Stephen King shake with fright?
Sex Movies to rival porn?   Adventure Movies!
Sci-Fi flicks that would make Stephen Spielburg jealous?
Love and Romance Movies?   Documentaries?
News reels?   Drama?   Soap Operas?
Commercials?   Police and Detective Cinemas?
Cowboy?

The range of Movies we can play on the screen of our minds goes on and on. Yet whatever plays governs our states, emotions, feelings, behaviors, skills, world-views, perceptions, health, and life. It determines what's *on* our mind. Yet the higher levels determine more important things—like *why* we watch what we do. We can even step back from the Movies that we play to take control of the productions, editing them, directing them, and even producing them. After all, it's our brain. It's the theater of *your* mind.

MovieMind is the newest work in the field of the cognitive sciences. It offers a user-friendly application of the models and patterns that allow you to *run your own brain.* And, of course, when you can do that, then you can *manage your own states* and *take charge of your own life.* Interested?

How would you like to be able to—

- Stop playing all B-rated Movies in your head?
- Film, create, and/or produce Grand Productions for your internal Theater?
- Take control of your Movies as editor, director, and producer?
- Run Quality Control checks on your Movies?
- Learn to step in and out of the Movies to enhance your own resourcefulness?

Everything in your life from your success, health, wealth, relationships, everything results from the Movies in your Mind.

Even your experience of all of these things, you experience as a set of images that play out on the screen of your awareness — as a Movie that you can edit and re-edit, direct and re-direct —once you know how to explore your Movie Mind and take charge of it. Otherwise, it will run B-Rated Movies and torture you day and night with such features.

When you wake up to your MovieMind and begin to take control of it—you have a set of tools for improving your thinking, reasoning, intelligence, communication skills, emotional intelligence, relationships, business success, health and fitness, and much more. It's not a panacea, it is rather the way your mind works and how you can work much more effectively with your mind.

*"He who directs his Cinema Mind
will get an Academy Award in resourcefulness."*

Tim Mackesey, Speech Pathologist

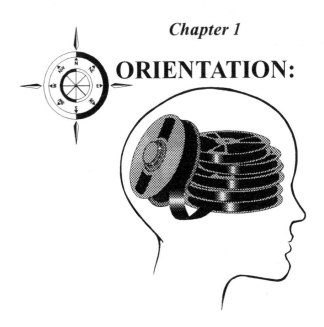

Chapter 1

ORIENTATION:

YOUR MIND AS A MOVIE

There's a surprising and intuitive thing that you'll learn in this book. It's a simple thing, yet profound. In one line, it is this:

> *We experience our "mind" as a Movie.* It's not that our mind *is* a Movie, it is only that we *experience* our mind's activities of thinking, feeling, knowing, deciding, valuing, and representing as a Movie.

"Surprising? Why is this surprising?"

It is *surprising* because there is no literal "movie screen" in our heads. Our brains are full of soft fleshy stuff and neuro-chemical substances, neuro-networks and pathways, but no movie screen.

It just *seems* like we *see* things in our minds, that we hear things in our minds, that we *feel, smell, taste, and fully experience* things *in our minds*. We close our eyes in sleep and we all could swear that we see again places from our childhood and scenes from our current home and place of work, and schools and that we see and hear and feel a world of people and friends and lovers and children. Yet that's the trick. It only *seems* like we are seeing, hear, and feeling that world. We are not. Not really.

It is in this sense that our Movie Mind is *surprising*. We all have this "feeling," if we can call it a feeling. We *feel* that "on the inside" we not only see, but that we also hear, feel, smell, and taste a whole world—a world we carry around with us in our minds. There's a name for this. Philosophers call it "phenomenology." That's a fancy way of talking about the *seeming* world that we live in inside our brains. Yet everything we have been learning in the past half century in the field of the neuro-sciences and cognitive-behavioral psychology informs us that none of this is real. Not externally. It is just our "sense" of reality, our phenomenological construct of reality. It is all made-up precisely because *we* invented it.

Does that mean there's no "reality" outside of our minds?
 Of course not.

The person who draws that conclusion misunderstands the distinction between our maps of reality and reality itself. What we map on the inside is just that, *a map,* a facsimile of external reality. Yet it is a map, or representation, of what we perceive to be on the outside, the territory "out there." Today, modern science continues to invent extra-neural devices to pick up and translate more and more of the energy manifestations "out there." This allows us to create more accurate, useful, and productive maps, or mental films, about what is "out there." And, the more accurate our maps, the more things we can *do*, the more places we can go, the more toys we can invent. This implementation in everyday life is how we can test our maps. We test our mental maps by seeing what we can now do or experience with them.

- After we map something, does it allow us to navigate further?
- Does it allow us to do new things, experience new things, create new things?

What we call science is dedicated to this entire endeavor of inventing better maps of the world. With a good map, our performances increase in effectiveness.

Intuitive

"So it is surprising. But why is it *intuitive?*"

It is *intuitive* that we think about our "mind," and our mental mapping of reality in terms of an internal Movie. *Intuitive* because it seems to be the way we all do it, the way we all experience the internal phenomenon that we call "mind." The way our neurological sense receptors abstract from the world and interpret it in our brains gives us the "sense" that we are seeing things inside our heads as we see, hear, feel, etc. things via our sense receptors. Of course, this is just a way of mapping our sense of mind. And in this it is simple.

"Okay, so it is surprising, intuitive and simple. But you said profound. How is any of this profound? It seems pretty simple to me. And besides, what practical value does any of this have?"

Great questions. *Mind as Movie* is profound because of what it now allows and empowers us to do. *Mind as Movie* gives us a practical way to "run our own brain" and thereby to manage our

states.
- How would you like to "run your own brain" and take charge of your states and experiences?
- Would that be beneficial to you?

By using the *Mind as Movie* frame, you can begin to run the Movies playing in our mental theater and rise up to become the editor and director of those Movies.

Medical science, psychiatry, genetics research, and other disciplines have dominated the scene by focusing our attention on trying to control our minds, states, emotions, experiences, and life at the *micro*-level of biology. "Take this pill!" They have been searching for the neuro-chemicals that govern consciousness. For this reason, psychologists, psychiatrists, and medical personnel are very quick at recommending pills rather than teaching people how to run their own brains, how to become the director of their own Movies.

"Why is that?"

There's lots of reasons. There's more money in it. The pharmaceutical companies promote it. It's easier. Just prescribe some pills and be done with it. It seems less complicated. No need to learn the mental and emotional competencies that are prerequisite for running your own brain, no need for self-awareness, self-understanding, or self-management— the E.Q. stuff (Emotional Quotient).

To "run your own brain" necessitates an emotional intelligence that fully accepts responsibility for the mental software programs that we run and that is willing to look inward to develop intra-psychic intelligence. Yet these are not the easiest skills to develop as both Daniel Goleman and Howard Gardner have noted in their respective studies. The art of running our own brain necessitates learning *how to work with* all of the images, sounds, words, sensations, feelings, emotions, etc. that play out on the screen of our mind.

This has been the challenge for hundreds, if not thousands, of years. *How* exactly do we work with all of the "stuff" of the mind? What is the "stuff" of mind anyway? How do we learn to take charge of the images, words, sounds, and feelings that go on inside us? As modern psychology began, numerous people offered different models about "mind" and its components which thereby suggested various approaches for taking charge of the chaos inside.

Yet there was a problem with every model. Most were too complicated. Freud introduced Greek mythologies as his template for understanding the psycho-dynamics. He introduced a new set of entities inside: Id, Ego, and Super-Ego. And his "gospel" was succinct, "Where there is Id, let there be Ego." The assumption that drove his model was the assumption that "Insight is inherently curative." If people understand, they are cured. Yet knowledge does not always cure. Do we not know more than we do? After knowledge, isn't there the question of implementation? Do we not then have to do—to put into action?

As psychology grew and models proliferated in the twentieth century, theorists and practitioners alike came to realize that in spite of the chaos on the surface there is rhyme and reason to why we think, feel, and do the things we do. There is a psycho-logic to it all. There are inherent drives and needs that we seek to fulfill. Maslow ordered these in a hierarchical form and separated survival needs from growth needs. Others tied *development* itself into human nature so that as Freud invented his psycho-sexual stages, others tied in psycho-social stages, psycho-cognitive stages, psycho-belief stages, psycho-cultural stages, etc.

Yet every model lacked something. Every model lacked the elementary components that are universally true for "mind." Yet, ironically, they were there from the beginning. In fact, the first psychologist of the modern age, Wilheim Wundt, knew of those elements as did all who followed him. But they didn't know what to do with them. Wundt specified the "senses," or the sensory systems, as the components of "thought." Yet try as he may, he didn't know how to turn these into "a periodic chart of the mind." That was 1890.

It took Korzybski in the field of General Semantics (1933) and then later a linguist (John Grinder), and a computer student (Richard Bandler) in the 1970s, to put it all together. From this came the field of neuro-linguistics and then later, neuro-semantics.

What was so new or different about NLP or Neuro-Semantics? These fields accepted the *macro*-level of the "senses" as the components of "thinking" and explored the magic of what we could do with these components. They explored the possibility that by changing the images, sounds, sensations, words, and the components of our inner awareness, what's on the "screen of our mind," we transform our thinking, feeling, and acting. So what happened? We found that it works. The deeper levels of neurology respond to the macro-level sense of our internal Movies.

This brings us back to another of the most intuitive things that we all know. *Change the way you think, and you transform your emotions, behaviors, and life.* It seems so simple. It happens to us all.

We think one way about something, and so we feel. Then we learn that our perception is completely wrong, that we misunderstand something. So we change our thoughts, change our mind, and then find that our feelings, speech, and behaviors also change.

Can "running our own brain" and taking control of our own lives be *that* simple?

If it is that simple, how is it that most of us do not feel in control of our own mental-and-emotional states?

* That we often struggle with our thoughts and feelings?
* That we try to make some thoughts go away, and they won't?
* That we try to stop feeling a certain way, and we can't?
* That we can recognize a pattern of thinking and feeling will undermine our health, sanity, and relationships, and yet we still fall victim to that same pattern repeatedly?

Why does it seem that "running our own brain" is one of the most challenging and difficult tasks that we face?

The answer to these questions is equally simply and intuitive when we think about it. The answer is that we have not been trained to know *how* to do it. We don't know *how to run the brain* to put ourselves in the best of states.

Yet now we can.

Recognizing that *we experience our "mind" as a cinematic Movie* uses a metaphor we all know and recognize. This metaphor invites us into a new level of awareness and skill in taking charge of running our own brains. The content of this book is very simple. Deceptively simple. You may be tempted to skip sections and exercises because assuming you already know something. Be aware of that seduction.

This book invites you to engage in drills and thought experiments that will allow you to actually test this model. Test it and see for yourself if the model works. The model of the mind presented here is experiential. Whether it is true or not, I don't know. I only know that most people have found it a powerful tool that works. This means that the test is in the experiencing, the doing, and the performing. My invitation here is for you to test it. Try it out. See what happens for you when you engage in the exercises.

The art of learning to "run your own brain" in this book is the art of taking charge of the cinema of your mind, what videos do you play on the screen of your consciousness, and how do you edit, direct, and produce your internal films. The design is to empower you to become the CEO of your own cinematic productions so that they will serve you well, enhance your life, make you more resourceful, and allow you to have the experiences that you desire.

If you're ready to do that, then *welcome to the Theater of Your Mind!* That's our next stop.

Chapter 2

WELCOME TO
THE CINEMA OF THE MIND

An Overview of New Movies for New Minds

"I have a Dragon that's been bothering me for years and I'm sick and tired of it."

Phil said this as he spoke up in a training that I was conducting on *Wealth Building.* We were doing the part about slaying and taming the *Dragons* that get in the way of our success. We do this to clear the pathway so that nothing will stop us from putting our knowledge and skills to good use.

"Good," I said, "Come on up here and let's play with that dragon in your mind and see what we can find. What do you call this dragon, Phil?

It's my fear-of-being-seen-as-inadequate dragon. That's what it is. I've lived with it all my life and I'm sick and tired of it.

You sound ready to go. Ready to tame that Dragon...
>No, I want to slay it.

Really? So, if you don't want to *fear* your inadequacies any longer, how would you prefer to feel about them?
>"Well ... ah ..." Phil was taken back for a moment by the question, but soon he said, "No... you don't understand. I don't want to be inadequate at all."

Really? So you want to be *The Renaissance Man,* or even better, *God?*
>"No, of course not. I just want to be ... ah..."

Super competent in all aspects of human experiences!
He picked up on the lightness of the comment,
>"Yeah, why not?!"

Phil, say hello to your dragon. Say hello to "Why can't I be Perfect and always Competent?" dragon. You do have a default program for perfectionism, don't you?
>Yes.

So, Phil, tell me this. If I were to peek into the theater of your mind and see what you see and hear what you hear when you make a mistake, what would I see going on in there?
>(Laughing) ... You wouldn't want to know. ... Okay, you'd see a picture of people pointing at me and mocking me and you'd hear their laughter ... and oh yes, there's my mother frowning and shaking her finger...

Is this Movie a horror Movie, comedy, sit-com, drama, melodrama, or tragedy? What kind of a Movie is this that you're playing?

Horror! Definitely a horror Movie.
It scares the hell out of you?

> Right. It makes me feel like a nothing, like a worthless bum ... like I can't do anything right...

Excuse me Phil, but it sounds like you're quoting the screenplay now. Is that what you're doing? Is there someone in the film actually saying these things, or is this the narrator's script describing the meaning of this Movie?

> Hummmm. I think it is the narrator's voice, my voice, and that I'm defining what this Movie means to me.

So you really like this Movie, right? (Using a bit of sarcasm.)

> Yeah, right! (Using even more sarcasm.)

So you have this B-rated Movie playing in the theater of your mind and it really makes life a party ... ("Yeah! Right!") which disgusts you and scares you ... so has it ever dawned on you to just *not* play this Movie?

> Well, not really. I never thought of it as a Movie. I never thought of it as something I could just turn off. How do I do that?

(Teasingly) Well, should I give you the secret? I mean, maybe you need this B-rated Movie? Maybe you get off on it. Maybe you really do like it and want it and long for it ...

Well, I tortured Phil awhile longer making sure he really was ready for a transformative change. But it began here. It began with the realization that the feelings and behaviors that sabotaged his best were functions of the Movie playing in his mind.

Your MovieMind

Your mind is like a Movie. When you "think," you play audio-visual scenarios on the screen of your mind. Plan a date with your loved one and what do you do? You make images of where you want to go and what that will sound like, feel like, smell like, and taste like, do you not? You edit a Movie of a fun night out. And when you think about other things, you also create mental Movies. You produce films of a relaxing vacation, of a challenging triathlelon, getting a raise, starting your own business, visiting Washington DC or the Pyramids of Egypt, or washing your car.

You do all of this because that's how we humans "think." We think in *images*—the things we see, snapshots, and moving pictures. We think in *sounds*—the background sounds at a circus or crowded mall, the music of a concert, the foreground sounds when standing at the foot of a waterfall, and the words and statements said. We think in *sensations*—the tactile sensations of touch, perhaps the smoothness of silk, the wetness of water, the rhythmic vibrations of a heart, and the internal sensations of relaxed or tense, excited or fatigued, the sensations of balance, dizzy or stable. We think in *smells* and *tastes*—strawberries, hot bread from the oven, a chicken coup on a farm, the fragrance of an aftershave lotion.

Our external *senses* operate as our internal *sensory channels* for our Cinema Mind. We have the unique and wonderful, and even magical, ability to literally *re-present* what we have experienced in our senses "on the inside of our mind." How this works, we really don't know. It has something to do with the transfer and transduction of information within our neuro-pathways. It really does not matter. That's just the hardware. The software of this fabulous bio-computer is the Movie on the screen of our mind. *That* it happens we can all testify to and that's what counts—our sense of our internal audio-visual Movies—our experience of our Cinema Mind.

"I don't know about this. I don't visualize very well at all."
Yes, many people are not *aware* of their internal Movies. How much *awareness* we have about our internal senses is another matter. That we create images and sounds and the other sensory information is simply a function of our nervous system, neurology, and brain. We even have parts of our brain that we call the visual cortex, the auditory cortex, the motor cortex, the associative cortex. When we open the brain and activate these parts of the brain with an electrical stimulus, the Movie begins. It typically sets off an association of representations so that we seem to re-experience seeing, hearing, smelling, etc.

While all of this is standard equipment for humans, typically, *most of us don't consciously notice this.* We just experience it. To *notice* our experience would be like focusing in on the control knobs or gauges on our television sets while watching a movie. Normally, we don't pay attention to the color, hue, sharpness, closeness, loudness, volume, tone, etc. Only when these factors move beyond the normal range, or until someone calls our attention to it, do we notice. Normally, we are caught up in *the content* of the movie.

Yes, that's our normal state. *We are caught up in the content of what's happening on the screen of our mind* That's why we don't notice the particular features of the cinema. It's only after we watch and enjoy a movie like *The Matrix, Jurassic Park, Star Wars, or The Wizard of Oz* that we even think about structural questions.

How did they do that?
What movie magic did they use to pull that off?

It looked so real, was that done by a computer? Typically we don't know the cinematic features that make up our mental Movies either. Caught up in the content, we're focused on the *what* rather than the *how*. This is an important point. It explains a strange phenomenon that frequently occurs. Many people find that when they begin to notice their cinemas, suddenly they can't see anything. Poof! The pictures just seem to vanish. This leads many to draw some strange conclusions.

"I just don't visualize."

"I kind of think I make pictures in my mind, but I can't see them."

These false conclusions are due to a simple fact. The person has confused making the pictures and responding to them (a typical *unconscious* process) and *consciously* noticing and controlling them. The secret to *seeing* what you *see* involves moving to a different level of mind—which is what we will do in a latter chapter.

Neurologically, if you can see, then you internally visualize. If you can hear, you have an internal sound track in your mind. If you have a body (like who doesn't?), you can feel internal sensations of experiences in your mind. The function of representing our internal seeing, hearing, feeling, etc. differs from the ability to become *consciously aware* that we are doing so. One is representation, which we all do. The other is conscious awareness of the representations—which is a learned skilled. It is a higher level of mind that we call *mindfulness*.

Conscious awareness of our internal sights, sounds, sensations, etc. is a developed skill necessary for the art of running our own brain. You can learn that skill, and you will learn it, if you give yourself to practicing the exercises in this book.[*1]

Welcome to the Movies of Your Mind

Stop where you are and look around and spot a human being. Any human being will do. Even an imaginary one will do. Now stop, look (don't stare!), and as you do, wonder, really wonder about this incredible fact:

> "There are Movies in that mind! There's a whole video arcade ready to be activated."

There is. What Movies are currently playing in that particular person's mind at this moment may not be immediately obvious (although they might). Yet you can count on this—there is something playing in the theater of that person's mind. In all of our minds, we are constantly entertained, tormented, delighted, scared, frustrated, relaxed, defeated, motivated, etc. by the Movie shows we watch on the inside. Count on it.

Count also on this. Everyday of your life as you move through the world, from when you get up in the morning, go to work, socialize with others, eat, exercise, drink, play, worry, laugh, and all of the other thousand things you do—you also are being induced into multiple states by the Movies playing in the showhouse of your mind.

The big questions with regard to all of this are these:

> What are you watching?
> What Movies are you playing?
> Are they Oscar winning productions?
> Do you give them a four-star rating?
> Or are they B-Rated Movies?
> Are you watching horror Movies, melodramatic films, sitcoms, worn out reruns, comedies, hero epics, or adventure?

These questions get right to the heart of the *quality* of our internal

Cinemas. Do they enhance or limit our lives? Do they put us in pleasant or unpleasant states? Do they bring out our best or our worst?

How can we tell *what* Movie is playing? Most of the time we don't have conscious awareness even of our own Movies. Yet because the Movies play and we respond, we have a clue about what's playing.

What are these clues?
Our responses. How we respond tells. It indicates what we must be watching. How we respond when we get up, go to work, interact with people, take on challenges, feel defeated by other challenges, etc.—our responses reflect the Movies playing on the inside. Our mental and emotional *states* tell on our mental cinemas. After all, our Movies put us into state.

We can therefore start with our mind-body *states* and backtrack to figure out what Movies we must be watching.
- What are you feeling?
- What's on your mind?
- What's your motivation?
- What do you feel like doing?
- What's your frame of mind?

Horror Movies tend to scare us, make us fearful, paranoid, expecting the worst to happen, etc. If that's where our head is at, we can expect to be distrustful, suspicious, full of fear, panicking, anxiety-ing, etc. As goes the Movie, so goes our state.

Are you full of lightness and fun and joy? Is everything a joke and silly? I bet there must be some comedies playing in your mind. Is it the Three Stooges? Candid Camera, America's funniest Home Videos? If this is where our head is it makes sense that it will come out in light-hearted fun and ludicrousness.

The Movies that we entertain in the theater of our mind govern how we respond. Some people are forever watching apocalyptical religious Movies and are forever ready to proselyte people to their narrow views. Others watch sex videos in the mind all day and that's what's on their mind, in their speech, and what drives their behaviors. Other watch violent, anti-vigilant pay-back revenge Movies. Some watch *Father Knows Best* and other movies of the idealistic family. Still others watch instruction videos on exercise routines. Then there are the Game Shows, "Who Wants to be a Millionaire?" "Weakest Link," "Survivors," etc. There are the detective shows, shows of live videos of cops chasing down crazed drivers and criminals, "Reality TV," etc. The choice seems endless: documentaries, travelogues, education, newsreels, animation, surrealistic, epic, etc.

What do you watch? What states do you typically find yourself in?

Movie Briefs and Channel Surfing
The next time you watch a movie preview whether on television or at a movie theater, watch it very carefully to notice how quick, jumpy, and captivating it is. Notice the rush of the pictures and sounds. Observe how the images sometimes seem to temptingly appear and instantly vanish leaving you interested in seeing more.

In a similar way *this is how our Mental Movies operate*—bits and pieces of scenes and ideas and thoughts and memories and imaginations flash on and off the screen of our mind very rapidly.

Or perhaps an even better metaphor for this is channel surfing. This certainly describes my experience of how I "think." It's as

if I can turn the channels of my mind and experience a rush of
sights-sounds-sensations coming from the various channels. I can
turn into or surf—

The History Channel	CNN or other News Channels
The Discovery Channel	The Imagination Channel
My Career or Work Channel	The Family Channel
My Love Life Channel	The Financial Channel

All I have to do is mention a class of activities or even a category
of awareness, and suddenly all kinds of snapshots and sound bites
pour in: Government, Taxes, Exercise, Health, Fitness, Mother,
Father, Race, Psychology, Economics, Theology, Justice, Trials,
etc. Our mental Movies are seldom a two-hour feature movie.
They are more typically 10-second movie briefs, quick flashes of
images and sounds.

New Movies / New Minds
Our *states* result from our mental Movies. After all, to watch a
movie we have to watch it from *some perspective*. We have to
identify with one of the characters and so be one of the players, or
we have to identify with the narrator, or some audience, or the
editor, or director, etc.

To watch is to take some perspective. And to take some
perspective is to receive *information* about *how to experience* the
movie. That's why the Cinemas that play out on the screen of our
mind are not neutral. As information, the signals send messages
to our bodies about how to feel and how to act. That's why even
when we watch a movie on television, we are ever so easily
seduced into the content and suddenly find ourselves trying to
apply the brakes as we sit on the couch or duck a punch or move
around to avoid falling off a cliff. The signals on the screen cue
our neurology and our motor programs.

We all know this. We watch a movie and go to bed and then toss and turn as we experience the Movie again and again, sometimes trying to write a new and better ending, sometimes going through the troubling scenarios again, and sometimes relating it to a personal event.

Movies, stories, dramas—the stuff of our internal cinemas put us into mind-body states. They elicit and trigger and stimulate mind-body states full of thoughts and feelings. That's why they affect our emotions, our health, our meanings. That's why they are not neutral.

> Given that our states result from our Movies, then what Movies would you prefer to watch so that you could experience a different set of states, feelings, perceptions, responses, and life-style?
>
> Do you have any of those recorded and stored in your video collection of films?
>
> Do you have permission to play those?

The Movies that play out on the screen of our minds primarily invite us to experience things from the role and perspective of *the actors* in those Movies. As we identify with various persons in the stories, we step in and suddenly it is as if we are there. This is the power of movies and stories. And it is especially the power of the Movies that play for the private showings in the theater of our mind.

These *key features* that make up our mental Movies is also what makes NLP and Neuro-Semantics so magical. Therefore as we become thoroughly acquainted with recognizing and using these features, we become skillful in mastering the Movie Matrix of our Mind. There is a *cinematography* of the mind and as we learn to play with these features of the cinema, we learn to take charge of our neuro-linguistic dynamics.

Exploring the Theater of Your Cinema Mind
Before we get into the details of your cinema mind or the principles of cinematography, we want you to become more familiar with your own cinema mind. Are you ready? Be sure you are in a place where you can read a bit and then stop, and "just think" about things.

In *the thought experiments* that we will do throughout this book, you will find them most productive if you have a quiet place and a notebook. These *thought experiments* will give you the chance to try things out, experiment with your own cinematography, and explore the landscape (mind-scape) of your inner theater. In these first experiments we want you to mostly just observe. Simply notice what happens and what thoughts arise.

The first experiment has to do with *an Embarrassment Flick.*
> Have you ever embarrassed yourself by really making a fool of yourself? Scan through the records of your memory ... perhaps back to childhood.
> Do you know what it's like to be embarrassed?
> What was that like for you?
> Where were you?
> How was it so embarrassing?

So what happened? Where did you go? Did you have any Embarrassment Film Flicks in your video-archives that you were able to access? Some people will have so many that their thoughts will bounce back and forth between this instance and then that one and then this other. Their thoughts will bounce around like thought balls in a lotto machine. Others will be able to focus in on one event, go right there, and possibly step so much into the

Movie that it may be hard to shake it off and step out. If that happens, you may even bring some of the feelings with you.

Others will find it difficult to find any instance of embarrassment. They may try on one memory after another, but then disqualify one after the other as not being good enough. Yet others may "think" about such, but not have the sense of "seeing" anything. For them, it may seem more like they are hearing the sound track but not seeing anything. Yet others may have no images or sounds but just a feeling or sense of the embarrassment.

The reason is because many people have a *favorite* or *preferred* sensory system: visual, auditory, or kinesthetic. Highly visual people will *see* the Movie. Highly auditory people will *hear* the sound track. This may focus on the actual sounds or on the words. Highly kinesthetic people learn by *feeling,* that is, *sensing.* Most of us, however, do all three to varying degrees.

The Fun Film
Let's play with our internal Cinema again. This time, think about some time when you really had a lot of fun. Pull up from your video library a *Fun Film.*
> Have you ever had a lot of fun doing something?
> Scan the library of your memory and settle on some time when you really enjoyed yourself, had a lot of fun, perhaps laughed a lot.
> The memory doesn't have to be the very best, just a memory when you were in a very pleasant state.
> Stop and do this now.

One factor about our internal cinemas that crucial to know about and understand is *how very, very quickly we scan* our Movies. Asking the kind of questions that we have can set off a cascade of images, memories, sounds, words, and feelings. The stream of our consciousness suddenly seems to become a rushing stream of intense rapids and whitewater.

In fact, it is this speed of our pictures flashing across the screen of our mind that may confuse us and even convince us that we are not seeing anything. For most of us, *holding an image still* so that we can more thoroughly examine it, play with it, and alter it will only come as a cinematic skill after some practice. Few people find that they can do that when they first start noticing their internal pictures.

Who's Running the Picture Show?

That our brains process the information from our senses—the sights, sounds, sensations, smells, etc., is simply a description of what brains do. We all have a brain with multiple cortexes, visual, auditory, motor cortexes that *process* information. That we can see a bowl of fresh ripe strawberries and recognize them as strawberries and cover them with whip cream and bring a fork with a big red juicy strawberry bathed in whipped cream to our mouth is information we can *process*, can we not? Yet in doing so, it affects our emotions, our feelings, our state.

That's the magic. As we process information on the screen of our mind, we *experience* sensations and emotions *as if we were inside the Movie.* How did you do with the strawberry description? Could you smell them? Taste them? See them? Hear them crunch as you bite down on them? What about the feeling of the cream and the strawberries inside your mouth? Are you doing it now? Stop and enjoy a Juicy Strawberry Film (of course, if you are allergic to strawberries, pick some other fruit).

This demonstrates something about human brains. We do not just *process information* as if we were un-involved computers or androids. When we process information, the information becomes *an internal Cinema inviting us to act out that information.* The information functions like a screenplay giving us instructions that direct us about how to feel and what to do. The information functions on several levels at the same time, and on one level it is also a director's command, "Lights, camera, action!"

This mind-body connection means that the Movies we play in the theater of our mind affects us emotionally and psychosomatically. So who's running the picture show? Our brains will just run whatever videos we have available in our video-archives unless we take charge. Taking charge means that we "run our own brains" and learn the art of mental cinematography. And that's what this book is all about.

In This Chapter:

- You pulled out three films from your video-archives and began exploring them: an Embarrassment film, a Movie of Fun, and a short clip about whipped cream covered Strawberries.

- As you continue to explore those audio-video productions in your mind, notice how your body responds. Our mental Cinemas put us "in state." They activate our somatic feelings (emotions) and motor programs. That's because we are neuro-linguistic creatures.

Chapter Endnotes

*1 One of the side effects of training in NLP and Neuro-Semantics is that people learn to pay attention to their internal Movies and so begin becoming aware of their internal seeing, hearing, feeling, etc.

NLP and the Movie Metaphor
Structure of Magic, Volume II

"The therapist listens and watches carefully—his task now is to teach the client to be totally congruent in his communications... The therapist acts as *a movie director* or a play director, coaching the client providing feedback, literally molding the client's body with his hands and words, instructing him in voice tonality and rate of speech until all of the client's output channels are representing the same or congruent paramessages." (1976, 64)

"Take the *Meta-Tactic 1— Movie/Play Director.* Here the therapist uses verbal instructions and kinesthetic instructions (molding the client's body into a more congruent posture)." (1976, 187)

Chapter 3

THE THEATER

The Physiology of
our Cinema Mind

"Okay, so it does seem like I see pictures in my head and that I sometimes have mental Movies going on in my mind. So where do these mental Movies play inside our heads, *where* exactly do we see these pictures? *Where* does this Movie show take place? How does this relate to the physiology of my brain?"

The answer is simple and mysteriously profound. The Movie takes place nowhere and yet everywhere.

We all have this "sense" of an internal cinema full of sights, sounds, sensations, smells, etc. and yet the Movie is just a metaphor. It's just a way of talking about things. The cinematic Movie that plays on the screen of our mind is not literal. We do not literally see anything in our head. We do not literally hear anything. We only "sense" that we do. It is phenomenological.

It only *seems* like you know what the Pyramids of Egypt look like and how that contrasts to a big red block that a child plays with or what King Kong would look like if he climbed the Empire State building. You only *think* that you *see* images in your mind.

Yet that is good enough.
It's good enough for "thinking." It's good enough for the thinking that we do when we engage in imagining, planning, reasoning, and using our intelligence to figure things out.

Our representational screen of awareness—what we "sense" inside in the theater of our mind is only a map that we use to navigate our way around the world. Actually, it is our only contact with the reality "out there." This "sense" of the see, hear, feel world gives us a *seeming awareness* of things, hence it is phenomenological.

As we simply speak about the *internal cinema* that plays out on the "screen of our consciousness" as we "think," and make sense of things, we experience our internal senses as we see, hear, and feel the Movie. We expand it to speak about the video-track, the sound-track, feel track, smell and taste tracks, the balance track (a sense of being upright or upsidedown, dizzy or clear, etc.) of our vestibular sensory system. So is there anything real or actual in our bodies that make any of this possible or is it all illusion?

Movie Time
Susan , you say you're afraid of public speaking. But I'm not convinced. How do you know you're afraid?

Because I get afraid every time.
Every time ... what? When you speak in public?
No, I never speak publically, I'm too scared to do *that.*

So you do *not* get afraid when you speak in public, you get afraid of *thinking about* speaking publically. Right?
Right.

So you've mastered the skill of scaring yourself with your thoughts.
Well, I don't like it when you put it that way. It sounds like I'm mental or something.

I hope so. It takes a lot of mind to be mental. ... If I'm understanding you accurately, just *thinking about* getting up and making a speech or saying something to a group creates fear inside.
Yes, that's right.

So if I were to peek into the Movie playing on the theater of your mind and see what you see that creates that fear and that activates your body to breathe faster and harder, what would I see? ... (pause) ... Think about a time when you really felt a lot of fear about public speaking ... has there ever been such a time?   ... Good, go there ... see what you saw back then.. That's right. Just notice what you're seeing and hearing ...
I see people staring at me and I know that I'll make a fool of myself, that I'm not good at this and then I imagine saying something wrong, I know that I shouldn't have done this.

Look at those people staring at you. Are you telling yourself that you'll make a fool of yourself? (Yes.) And notice the tone you use in saying that, is it a sexy tone of voice?

(Laughing) No. Not at all. I'm scolding myself.

Scolding yourself? That sounds like fun. And how loud is that voice? Just notice. And where is that voice coming from? Is it coming from inside your head or from around you or above you or...

It's all around. And it's very loud.

Panoramic? It fills up the whole atmosphere inside that Movie.

Yes. That's terrible.

Well, if you don't like it, reduce that voice ... turn down the volume until you can just barely hear it and put it as having one source ... maybe in your little finger. There you go.

Where are the words about "not being good at this" and that you "shouldn't have done this" ... where are those words coming from? Where in the Movie do you put those words? Are they yours? Someone else's?

I don't know. It's my words... it's like I am seeing myself on stage and I'm in the audience and I'm judging myself.

So you are popping in and out of the Movie. One minute being the presenter, then popping out into the audience to be a critic, then back into the presenter's position?

Right.

So the voice of judgment is coming from *the you* out there in the audience judging yourself.

Yes, that's right. I never noticed that before.

Well, have you ever felt playful and teasing, maybe a little bit of a flirt... yes, give me the eyes of flirting. There you go. And listen to the voice in your head when you are a tiny bit seductive in saying, "Dinner is ready." Or something even more sexy, "E equals MC squared." You can't say that in a flirting way and just relax into that kind of a state and be in the presenter's role in that mental Movie and just look into the eyes of the people there ... engaging each pair of eyes and just twinkling your playfulness as you say things ... and as you imagine editing your Movie in this way, just how much more resourceful do you feel?

It's weird. I feel that I could actually do that.

Well, don't run that Movie in your mind when you think about public speaking. Who knows, then you'd be sharing your ideas and being more successful and forgetting about judging yourself and just doing significant things that makes a difference in the world ... and you're too serious to be playful in that way, weren't you?

The Neurological Foundations
Yes there is a neurological foundation to our states of consciousness and the particular kind of consciousness we humans experience. This means that there is a relationship between *the kind of bodies* we have and the kind of internal experience that we report when we talk about our "mind" and the things on our minds.

So if the Cinema of our audio-video-sensate Movies occurs without a literal "screen," then how is it that we think we "see" things? How does this work?

It begins with our *neurology*. Our Cinema Mind is a *neuro-cinema*. How all of this actually works, we don't know. While we have made tremendous breakthroughs in neurology and in the neuro-sciences, what we know about the architecture of the brain is still in its infancy. And how brain gives rise to *mind*, well that's yet another mystery and one that we are far from understanding.

What we do know is that all of our neurological structures are designed as an information processing miracle. It begins with the DNA genetic structure that encodes the most fundamental information that gives instructions for how cells are to grow and divide and through that splitting to specialize to become all of the different organs of our embodied experience. We are *neural creatures*; we live an embodied life inside bodies that have boundaries and that can tell the difference between "me" and "not me." Our nervous tissue maps or models the energies "out there" in the world and transduces that information through the sense receptors to become bio-electrical-impulses along neuro-pathways and then chemical exchanges at the molecular level.

In this way we use our multiple nervous systems (central, autonomic, peripheral, immune, etc.) along with our sense receptors, and basic "senses" to create a map of the territory out there, a map that allows us to navigate our way through life. Yet typically we don't experience it so much as a map, but more as a film, as an internal Movie. We experience our neurological mapping as an audio-visual sensory track. and, it is this Movie that is important.

At least it is important in terms of how we *sense* things, order our Movie-map of reality, and "think," "reason," and figure things out. At least it is important in how we experience the "things" (i.e., ideas, beliefs, etc.) of the mind-and-emotions. Because, it's through our thinking-and-feeling system (all the stuff that we do inside our head) that governs our behaviors, speech, skills, and personality.

So we start with our *neurological map of the world.* We sense things in terms of the structures of our body—in terms of sights, sounds, smells, sensations, tastes, equilibrium, etc. After many more levels of abstraction, we experience the "sense" of internal sight, sound, sensation, smell, etc. in such a way that it seems like we are *re-presenting* what we saw, heard, felt, etc. We do not *literally* have these sensory modalities on a literal screen in our mind, but it *seems* as if we do. It seems like we have images, sounds, sensations, etc. on the inside. This creates our basic *awareness* of the world.

This internal "sense" of the sensory modalities which we experience as a seeing-hearing-feeling Movie is made up of our visual, auditory, kinesthetic representations. This is how we "map" or film the world.

The Building of the Neuro-Theater
It is *not* the actual neuro-pathways, the firing of neurons that trigger the exchange of chemical messages that create comprise "thought" or "emotion." Thought and emotion arise as emergent properties from the entire system and should not be equated with a singular biological event. We do not find consciousness at the molecular or sub-molecular level. These are but the hardware out of which arises the macro-level experience that we call *awareness.* Today when we watch the actual functioning of the brain as it "thinks," we speak about the firing of cell assemblages—billions of neurons firing.

We should not think of *consciousness, thought, awareness, memories, imagination, beliefs, understandings,* etc. as an immediate brain function localized in a particular meaning. It's not like that. Awareness is a composite experience arising from the entire system. Yet it is in using all of the parts of our brain-body nervous systems that we are able to create the *sense of an internal Movie.*

The neurological mapping from the external world to our internal world occurs as our sense receptors selectively focus on a small amount of information and then translate that information into neurological information.

In any kind of map-making, we map only the most crucial features of a territory. We leave lots of things out, we don't need to know everything. In map-making we also have to generalize, summarize, and abstract to create summaries of things. We round things off to get a general sense of the territory, the landscape in which the action occurs. We also alter, change, or distort other things which is why even grossly exaggerated caricature maps can provide valuable help in getting from one place to another. It's the structure that counts. If it is similar to the territory, it will do.

Consider the neurological mapping of light from which we get our sense of vision. What impinges upon our eyes is electromagnetic radiation, light. We cannot see that energy for what it *is*, so we distort it via our rods and cones. This gives us the sense of "color." Our two eyes give us the sense of "depth." Of the 100,000,000 light sensitive cones, we only have 1,000,000 nerve impulses to the brain. So we reduce what we receive at a rate of 1/100. That leaves a lot out. It changes the form from electromagnetic radiation to cell activation, to a nerve impulse, to the exchange of neuro-transmitters, etc. What goes in at one end (the eyes) does not show up at the other (the brain).

Mapping a Movie to Navigate By
Our neurological mapping changes, deletes, generalizes, distorts things to give us a "sense" that we can use. In this way we end up with a map or Movie *of* the territory. We end up with *a*

phenomena-neurological map. When we become aware of it, we have the internal sense of a map. This gives us a sensory-based internal Movie that we can now play in our mind.

> Video #1: "I see a dog; I hear the dog barking, I feel the dog's soft hair and wet nose, I smell the dog..."
>
> Video #2: "Bill was furious about the report and tore it in two shortly after I handed it to him. Then he raised his voice and asked if it was a joke or if I really didn't care about working there any longer."

Here are the Movies. These Movies are not very detailed or clear. They only give us a general idea of a scenario. Yet we have a "sense" of the visual features, we have a sense of the sound track, and of the feel track, smell track, taste track, and balance track. Yes, I know this sounds really weird. Theater owners are still working on installing other sensory tracks to the audio-visual tracks.

> Yet in the mind—in the theater of human consciousness *we have multi-dimensional tracks in all sensory systems.*

You might have noticed that in the last chapter when we described big red juicy strawberries covered with whipped cream. If you had any sense of what that would taste or smell like, then you used your smell and taste tracks. Of course, this is what makes the internal Cinematic World of mind so magical. We can represent these sensory features and step into the Movie so that all of our neurology responds.

As a preview of things to come, *when you wake up to the existence and power of your Cinema Mind, you'll discover that you have cinematic power.* In the internal world of your mind —you can do all kinds of wild and wonderful things to create the kind of Universe that you want and that brings out your best.

Installing Sound Tracks in Silent Movies

We not only attach sounds, noises, music, tones, pitches, etc. to our cinema, we also attach a sound track of words. This allows us to hear the words that the people in the Movie say as well as our own internal Movie narrator and/or critic.

For "mind," this offers even more internal magic. We can (and do) encode our mental Movie not only with one sound track, but multiple tracks. We not only have our own voice saying things, we can have other narrative voices occurring: mom's, dad's, a teacher, a religious figure, a vague historical narrator, etc.

We make our mental Movies first out of our "senses" (what we see, hear, feel, smell, etc.) and sensory-based language (simple, empirical language). Yet this is just the beginning. We never stop with that. We then create more abstract ideas to invent higher level concepts and knowledge systems. As a result, *the words* in our sound tracks become richer and more complex. This can change the quality and even the very nature of the Movie.

Consider the language track going on in an infant or small child's mind. You can even hear it in a child's tonality, can you not?

> "See doggie. See Dick and Jane. Look! Doggie is running after the duckie!"

The same scenario playing in the Movie of the mind of an adult undoubtedly has a different set of words and tone in the sound track.

> "When we brought home the first puppy that we got for the children, the pup was full of excited energy especially when the neighbor's duck came into his line of sight...."

The *visual scenario* that we represent and "see" in the theater of our mind is just part of the *content*. The *auditory sound track* supplies more of that content (the words being spoken by the actors). Or it can operate at a higher level as the narrator's explanation about the Movie. In the latter case, the words set a frame *about* the Movie. If the sound is playing loud and pervasive circus music while the Movie seems like a serious business meeting, funeral, or race riot, our experience of it will differ if we have suspenseful dramatic music, rock-n-roll, classic, etc.

Movie Frames
When we introduce words and language into our Movie, we move to a higher level of production. Now our words can not only consist of the actor's lines, they can also be used to frame the meaning of the Movie. This gives us the actor's sound track as well as a narrator's sound track. And the words we use in the sound track influences how we *frame* things. Childish words and tones set one frame while academic words, journalist terms, poetry, rap, etc. set other frames. Our choice of language, style, tone, etc. set frames about the Movie and cues us about how to encode and frame the Movie.

When I look at the puppy chasing the duck or jumping upon the child with its wet nose and licking its face ferociously, what language plays out *inside* the Movie, what words do I hear playing out as if *narrating* the Movie, and what words may an *editor's* voice be saying, or another spectator to the Movie?

> From *inside* the Movie, the child is laughing and giggling. From *the back* of the Movie, my voice is sorting for the degree of the dog's roughness or playfulness and how the child is experiencing it. "Just as long as its play and fun; I don't want anyone to get hurt."
> From *the edge* of the Movie, an editor's voice says, "Zoom in on the shot of the child's laughing and delight."

Because our *linguistic mapping* of the world in our Movies shifts us to higher levels, this gives us our primary ways of *framing* the meaning of our cinemas. Every Movie screen, play, and picture occurs inside of a frame. In fact, we use the frames to contribute to the meaning of the cinema.

At *the editorial level* we frame the cinema. How much the Movie fills the screen or rescinds into the background, how clear or fuzzy the images are, how bright or dim ... these facets of the Movie create a certain frame. The cinematic features of how we use the curtain, rising it or lowering it, when we see the screen as a flat picture, a movie, a 3-D holographic image, inside or outside, with borders or panoramic —these are editorial distinctions that we can make about the Movie.

We can do the same with words. What we call it is, the labels and terms we use, governs how we encode the Movie. Real, not real; vivid, dull; interesting, boring; significant, irrelevant; about me, not about me; escapism, science fiction, documentary; educational, entertainment. The terms we use about the movie, or any feature of the movie, enables us to frame it with different meanings. Some framing affects perception, others affect conception. Both influence feelings.

Bodies—Neuro-Linguistic Information Processing Systems
Because our sensed mental Movie arises as a neurological process within our physiology as embodiment persons, all of our internal Movie making is inescapably *neuro-linguistic.* What we represent, map, encode at the sensory-based and evaluative levels —we experience and feel *in our body.* The words we use are impactful and significant inside our mind-body system as director and editorial cues for the Movie. That's why we can use both, *the tools of mind* (words, language, linguistics, symbols) and *the tools*

of the body (movement, posture, breathing, etc.) to improve, correct, and transform the Movies that govern our everyday experiences. All of these factors make up our neuro-cinema.

From the DNA coding in our genes, to the neurotransmitters, peptides, glands, central nervous system, immune system, all the way up to our brain anatomy and then to the way our "mind" functions to encode and decode data, we operate as information processors. We take in information, transduce it to a form our body can use and then respond to it.

This is what gives us "life" and separates life from non-life. We respond to the world and do so by abstracting information from the world, encoding it as a map, and responding according to our model of the world.

Most of all this information processing of inputs and outputs occurs outside the level of awareness—in our *embodied* flesh. It is part of our "cognitive unconscious" (Lakoff and Johnson, 2000) and cannot be accessed. Some of it lies below awareness and can be brought into consciousness. Consciousness is a narrow band of awareness severely limited by how much it can hold in awareness at any given time. George Miller (1956) described it as the "magic number 7 plus or minus 2" in his classic paper by that title and this suggests the numbers that make up that limit.

All of our neurological processes make up *the theater, the neuro-theater* in which we create our Movies. That's why our internal Movies *seem* to be so similar to what we experience with our external senses and sense receptors. As we use our eyes and ears and skin for detecting what is "out there," so we use these three primary modes of awareness as our sensory tracks. We also use our tongue, nose, and inner ear for detecting where we are in space and for moving toward a sense of balance. And there are other sense receptors as well.

This means that we primarily "think" in terms of our primary *senses.*   We think in terms of our sensory systems for representation. NLP describes this as the sensory representational systems: visual, auditory, and kinesthetic.   Howard Gardner's theory of multiple intelligence describes it as the seven modalities of intelligence.   Some of these modalities are primary systems: visual-spatial, bodily-kinesthetic, musical-rhythmic, while others involve more abstract or conceptual systems: verbal-linguistic, logical-mathematical, inter-personal, intra-personal.

The Condition of the Neuro-Theater
Governs the Energy in the Movies
We all know what happens when we let ourselves get out of shape, lazy, fatigued, and/or when our bodies are suffering from a cold, an illness, or some disease. When we feel down, lethargic, and unfit physically—our mental Movies suffer. Surely you've noticed that. When we don't feel good physically, our internal cinemas become darker, gloomier, less lively, less vigorous. This mind-body-emotion connection simply highlights the nature of our mental theater as a *neuro*-theater. And it is affected as much by the condition of our body as by the contents of the movie show.

Experiment with this and test it for yourself. Stop where you are right now and do this. Slump over and look down. Loosen all your muscles and relax into that downward slump... almost as if you could fall into the floor. As you do, constrict your breathing so that it becomes very shallow and restrained. As you now keep looking down to your right scanning the floor, try to re-call a vital picture show of energy and vitality and playfulness while holding that posture.

Difficult? It is for most people.

Now, do this. Sit up in your chair or even better, stand up. Stretch a bit, breathe in deep full breaths, look around the room and then up. Bounce on your toes ... and tighten and release the muscles in your legs, arms, back, etc. Now call forth a vital picture show from your archives of video memories, one of energy, vitality, and playfulness while looking up and bouncing on your toes every once in awhile.

How was that? Easier? Yes, the body does affect the mind just as the mind affects the body.

In This Chapter:

* We've discovered the intimate relation between mind-and-body and how that the very structure of our body, nervous systems, and brain-body system to process information—which we do by using our external senses as our internal sensory modalities for representing things as a Movie show.

* The nature of our bodies relates to and plays a determinative role in the nature of our thinking, reasoning, understanding, and using symbols as we map the world.

"You create an entire picture of movie in your mind, and in that picture you are the director, you are the producer, you are the main actor or actress. Everyone else is a secondary actor or actress. It is your movie."

Don Miguel Ruiz
The Four Agreements (p. 52)

Chapter 4

CINEMA MIND AT WORK

Turning Thoughts and
Words Into Mind Movies

Just how does our Cinema Mind work?
How do we translate things of the mind other than
immediate sights, sounds, sensations, smells, etc. into our
mental Movies?

At the level of sensory *re-presentation* it's obvious that we take
what we see "out there" and create our sense of internally seeing.
We take what we hear on the outside and make it our sound track
on the inside. We don't understand *how* it all works, but we
somehow do create a facsimile of our sensory systems within our
mind. And that's what we experience as our Movie.

This juxtaposition between external and internal seeing, hearing, and feeling can be tricky and deceptive. This arises, in part, due to *the speed* at which we switch back and forth from inside to outside.

To get a sense of that, stop and look all around where you are. As you "come to your external senses" just seeing, hearing, feeling, smelling, and tasting your immediate environment, try holding on to them as you notice how quickly internal images come and go. Notice what pops into your mind as you read the following ...

The Eiffel Tower in Paris.

Your fifth grade classroom.

Rocky calling for Aderin in the "Rocky Movies," —"Yo! Adrein!"

Mona Lisa's smile.

Bugs Bunny chomping on a carrot, and saying, "What's up, doc?"

Your childhood home at ten-years of age.

Was that a trip or what?

Yet that's how *mind* works ... how the *cinematic nature* of mind works. Pictures, images, sights, sounds, sensations, smells, and tastes popping in and out of our Movie theater in milliseconds. The Movies we run in our mind are hardly ever full-length two-hour Movies. More commonly they are two-second scenarios. When we experience a three-minute one, we are in deep trance!

All of this becomes a bit more complicated when we deal with more abstract ideas. Yet here too we somehow *make sense* of things by literally *making sense* of things. That is, we take words and *track over* from those words to create visual, auditory, and kinesthetic *sense* on the screen inside our minds. As noted earlier, we can easily *make sense* out of statements like,

> "The brown dog jumped up on Jim's lap and licked him in the face."

You probably found that you could not help but quickly translate those images onto the screen of your mind? Wasn't that easy? Didn't you comprehend those words about as quickly as you ready the words? That's because you could *make sense* of them... you could *representationally track them* directly to your mental Movie screen.

But try to do that with,

> "Objective consideration of contemporary phenomena compels the conclusion that success or failure in competitive activities exhibits no tendency to be commensurate with innate capacity ..."

What did you do with that one? Were you able to make visual sense of that? If so, what images did you see? Did you make any auditory sense of it? Kinesthetic sense? It was more difficult, wasn't it?

Why is it more challenging? Because the words themselves are not easily translated into see-hear-feel audio-video-terms. They were too abstract. Too vague. We could not easily create "sense" representations with them. It would be easier to representationally track the words, "The race is not always to the swift, the battle is not always to the strong..." Once we have that on the screen of our mind, then we can more easily put in a narrator's voice or the caption on the screen, "time and chance happens to them all." In doing so we have made, or created, *"sense"* and translated the previous statement.[*1]

Reading, communicating, understanding, comprehending, and a host of other similar experiences depend on our ability to *representationally track* words and ideas. If we can make an internal mental Movie of what we're reading, what someone is saying to us, or what we are seeking to understand in a field of study, we learn, know, and comprehend the meaning.

This means that learning, intelligence, comprehension, information, and a host of other experiences are functions of our ability to create internal Movies. If we can't create a Movie—we can't really understand something. (This will be the subject of the later chapters.)

Would you like to accelerate your learning skills?
Would you like to enhance your intelligence?

These experiences are not as mysterious as we often think. Fundamentally they work by the simple process of *representationally tracking* symbols and creating an internal cinema in the mind. If you can do that, then you "know," "comprehend," have "intelligence," are "smart," etc.

But that's the problem. People, books, and programs throw all kinds of abstract terms, words, and ideas at us leaving us in a cinematic fog. We can't make a Movie out of *those* words and terms. What are we to do? If we only had a way of reducing the fog, seeing through the vagueness, or chasing away the abstractness. Well, the good news is, we do.

Movies in the Zip Drive
In a computer, a zip drive condenses the information in a file —compresses the information to create a zip file. Then sending these files back and forth are a hundred times faster than regular files. Later you just un-zip them and all of the information is there.

A similar thing happens with the way we process mental Movies. At first we film at the speed of life. We film the things that happen and the talk we hear according to our first experience and so record it all at the rate and speed at which they happen. But later ... later when we remember those events, we recall and re-present them to ourselves at a more accelerated rate. We skip over the parts that drag along and zoom right into the important parts. In this way, *we engage a mental zip program,* so to speak. This allows us to zoom right through our Movies, skipping the slow and boring spots and getting right to the heart of things.

When we think about the nasty confrontation we had with our boss, we zip right through everything that happened at work that day and get right to the moment where he yells at us. At that point, we slow everything down and put the film on endless repeat (as if we didn't have anything better to do with our brains!). Then we see constant instant replays ... which we juice up by making it bigger, closer, and louder. Of course, this naturally makes us feel worse ... so we play it again.

When we finally stop that non-sense, we zip the whole piece up into a file and we don't even have to un-zip it the next time. Now the whole zip file is re-labeled: "The Worst Day of My Life at X Company and with Mr. Benton." Now the zip file can zoom into and through our mental theater in a nanosecond and carry the full wallop.

Then one day many years later someone mentions something that outside-our-awareness reminds us of "Mr. Benton" and ... Pow! Suddenly we feel awful. Terrible feelings rush in.

"What's wrong?" the other person asks.

    "I don't know. We don't know what happened. I just feel

a pain right here in my stomach. I can hardly breathe."

And we don't. The Zip Movie plays at warp speed and we don't even know what's playing in the theater of our mind. We only know the physical wallop we get from it. The punch. The *feeling impact* of the Movie is now encoded kinesthetically in our muscles and internal organs. It's become a *neuro-semantic reaction* that mostly operates unconsciously. Of course, that's why part of the process of directing our own Movies sometimes involves *un-zipping* the old Movies and teasing out the meanings, frames, and dynamics that have become streamlined in this way. [This is the structure of PTSD.]

Zip Files in Action

Outwardly, Terri was the kind of person who always seemed positive and full of energy and optimism. She had lots of plans and big visions for her life. When joking there were times when there was a bite to her humor, almost sarcasm but never quite. She said it was just teasing. So when she asked for a consultation I was a bit taken back.

I asked about what she wanted and she began to let me see a very different person. A person who kept up a persona about herself and one that did not fit her internal reality. While externally she seemed outgoing, friendly, and optimistic, internally she was fearful of people, distrustful of people, she hated "politics," didn't believe in people, didn't have a lot of hope for herself, feeling lots of stress over the disparity between her internal reality and her external presentations, incongruent, and the list went on and on.

This was a side to her I had never seen. There was some hurt inside that was festering and creating all of this. The question was how to elicit it in such a way that she could talk about it without going into that state and getting caught up in those strong negative emotions. With as much compassion as I could convey, I said,

"You've really been hurt ... hurt deeply ... hurt by someone you loved with all your heart ... and probably hurt in a way that shocked the hell out of you... and I don't know...

Suddenly she was in tears. The context of wanting to make a change along with the context of confiding and compassion was enough to allow the old Horror Movie to be called forth. And it came quickly.

"That's right... and this Movie in your mind has never gone away ... it has been plaguing and tormenting you for years ... perhaps for all your life ... and now, instead of trying to push it away because you know that doesn't work, it never has worked, it has only created an internal fight ... so now just welcome it in ... just welcome it in as an old Movie in your mind ... and let it play on the theater of your mind ... as you step back from it and just watch it ... watch that little girl in that old Movie... a Movie that *that* little girl gave too much meaning to and misunderstood and somehow personalized because I want you to watch it for the last time ... because now you can update that Movie, slow it down, face it with new adult resources and when we're done, you can either file it away in the room of Old Movies or even let it dissolve into nothing..."

In a later chapter I'll give you the process for updating old Movies, re-editing them, and de-commissioning them. For now, it's important to know three things. First, the things in our mind-body-emotions are just old maps. Just mental maps. And as maps, they are only as good as the thinking and reasoning that created them. They are not real, they are just maps. Second, welcoming them allows us to change them and control them whereas rejecting them or denying them infuses them with more power. Third, they can rush and zip into our mind within the realm of awareness or outside of awareness in a nanosecond.

The Rush of Images in Our Movies

Consider what happens when you go to the Movies and see a new release. Whenever we see a Movie for the first time ... as with real life ... there are so many things to see, to notice, and to pay attention to that it all seems to go by so fast. Whoosh! We can't take in all the jumble of images, sounds, sensations, feelings, meanings, etc. the first time. The first time our unconscious selective filters kick in and we see what we are most prepared and oriented to see.

But watch the movie a second time. Review the video-camera that recorded the real life event. And suddenly we are able to see *so much more*. We all experience this phenomenon. We say, "I didn't see that before!" Sometimes what we didn't see or hear or sense the first time comes as a shock, "Was *that* there before?"

Engineer turned semanticist, Alfred Korzybski compared the *structure* of primary states full of emotions and energy (which he called first-order abstractions) and the higher or meta-states (second-order abstractions). He used the analogy of *watching a movie*. In watching a film, we can either just go ahead and *experience* the drama and movement of the movie or we can deal with it as if a director or editor. We can keep stopping the movie to look at its *structure and form* so that we can then draw conclusions about it's meaning and nature. The content at the immediate experience gives us movement, drama, and emotion. The structure and form at the higher level gives us understanding, analysis, awareness, and choice.

Korzybski noted that when our internal pictures operate as a dynamic and ever-shifting *movie*...

> "... our 'emotions' are aroused, we 'live through' the drama; but the details... are blurred. ...The picture was 'moving,' all was changing, shifting, dynamic, similar to the world *and* our feelings on the unspeakable levels. The impressions were vague, shifting, non-lasting, and what was left of it was mostly colored by the individual mood..."
>
> "But if we *stop* the moving film ... and analyze the static and extensional series of small pictures on the reel, we find that the drama which so stirred our 'emotions' in its moving aspect becomes a series of slightly different static pictures, each difference between the given jerk or grimace being a *measurable* entity..."
>
> "The *moving* picture represents the usually brief processes going on in the lower nerve centres, 'close to life', but unreliable and evading scrutiny. The *arrested* static film which lasts indefinitely, giving *measurable* differences ... allows analysis and gives a good analogy of the working of higher nerve centres, disclosing that all life occurrences have many aspects... The moving picture gives us the process; each static film of the reel gives us stages of the process in chosen intervals." (*Science and Sanity*, p. 292)

Here Korzybski describes the nature of our internal computations as we experience them at different levels of our brain. This allowed him to separate them into two kinds. He noted how that they correspond to the levels of our brain information processing. The thalamus processes the ever shifting nature of things at the immediate (and lower) levels. That differs from the way our neo-cortex processes information in a more static form.

> "The cortex receives its materials as elaborated by the

thalamus. The abstractions of the cortex are abstractions from abstractions and so ought to be called abstractions of higher order. ... The receptors are in direct contact with the outside world and convey their excitation and nerve currents to the lower nerve centers..." (p. 290)

We go from lower to higher brain processing. At the level of the *thalamus,* everything seems like a jumble of sights, sounds, and sensations.   At this level we experience lots of movement, sensations, and feelings. Yet we can learn from these lower level images. So, as we send these images up the levels, they are "re-educated" by the—

"... development of poise, balance, and a proportional increase of critical judgement and so 'intelligence' at the higher levels. These higher level abstractions have *lost* their *shifting* character and are further removed from the outside world." (p. 291)

This explains why, when we are experiencing our Movies, the lower level of mental processing, we experience it as information quickness, fluctuations, and movement.   It's all a flurry of activities. This is what creates our emotionality and reactivity. This explains why it's much more difficult to *directly* control our "thoughts" at this level.   It explains that when we send our "thalamic material" (our cinematic Movies) up to the higher processing levels we are then able to slow down our images, direct them, edit them, and take charge of them. We're operating at a higher level. At that level, we can make a snapshot and just hold the image. This gives our images more stability.

Now we know *why* it sometimes seems that we have to keep playing a B-rated Movie over and over in our mind. We do so to fully understand what in the world is happening or has happened.

First exposure came too quickly. We need to review it and so we do, in our mind. But the trick is *not* to just replay the video as it happened. If we do that, the Movie can get caught in an endless loop. Then we can feel stuck, even compulsive about it.

The trick is to *step out* of the Movie and to send the information upstairs. When we can process it not only in the thalamus, but also in the higher evaluative cortex, we can then step back from the Movie and re-educate it. Then, from the level of directing our own mind, we can give it poise, balance, and proper evaluation.

Cinema Mind at the Higher Levels

Just as there are actual neurological levels of information processing in your brain, so there are *levels of thought in your mind.* That's why you can *think* about your thinking. You can experience *feelings* about your feelings. This meta-cognitive ability (as it is called) arises from our self-reflexive consciousness. We *reflect* on the previous products of our brain-mind. And every time we do, we create another *layer* of awareness or of mind.

These second thoughts and third thoughts set the frame for your mental Movies. If you play a trauma scene (yours or someone else's) from within the Movie as the key actor of the action, then you will experience more trauma. If you play it from the position of the perpetrator of the evil, you play the villain. That's all well and good. No harm *if you know* what you're doing and that you're doing it.

Mindfulness, in this sense, is curative and preventive of semantic harm.

But if you don't know ... if you are not mindful ... if the Movie is just playing *and* you think it's real (after all, your body is getting the signals) then semantic harm will occur. Then, *for you,* it is not just a Movie. It is not just thoughts. Not recognizing the map-like nature of thoughts causes you to *frame the thoughts as real*—and that creates the internal harm and danger. The semantic frame *"This is real!"* informs your body and neurology to respond as if to actual danger.

The structure of the experience, in this case, is frame-by-implication. Now you are assuming that what you see-hear-feel-smell-and-taste from within the mental Movie is real. This second-thought is what *makes it so* to you. In this, your *second thoughts* are more important than your first thoughts. The thoughts you have *about* the first thoughts construct the mental contexts or frames *about* the first ones. The first ones are *content*, the second ones function as *structure or context.*

In thinking *about* our Movies and the experiences we have inside our Movies, we *layer* thought and feeling upon thought and feeling. This creates states *about* our states, or meta-states. And these determine the form and meaning of our internal cinema world. What does the trauma Movie mean? It determines your second thoughts, your reactions to those first reactions.

"This is the way life is ... full of pain, hurt, trauma and always will be."

"This is about me—I don't deserve anything better."

"This is just a record of something I once experienced, but no more."

"This is a warning about how harm can occur."

"This is the past and I refuse to let it define my future."

A Movie is never fully defined or described by the events it records. What it means depends on the frames we put around it. This is where taking control of our meta-states frames gives us new freedoms and powers for meaning-making.

The Code of the Higher Levels

As we move up the levels of mind, we create higher level meanings about things. We set frames as we classify things in certain categories. Yet in doing this, we use a different kind of language. Language becomes increasingly more abstract and conceptual as we move up the levels. The sensory-based empirical language of the brute facts of the world fade out and give rise to more evaluative language.

Now we do not see a man rolling his eyes and tensing his muscles and quickly jumping to his feet at a conference table during a meeting and raising his voice, "I've had enough of this non-sense!" We do not see him shove his chair backwards or pound the table with his fist and then quickly move to the door and slam it as he goes out.

No, we only say, "Mr. Thompson lost it in the meeting and acted like a fool."
Do those words give us a screen play regarding how to represent things? Try it. Try to take *just those words* and make a mental Movie of them. Do not use the words from the previous paragraph. If you succeed, then congratulations on your ability to hallucinate.

What do the words "lost it" and "acted like a fool" translate to in sensory images and sounds? They are very abstract terms. And we can use even more abstract terms. "Mr. Thompson was very unprofessional at the meeting today." Try to *track* those words representationally *just* using them. You can't. You can not without hallucinating and inventing your own film for "unprofessional."

Yet the abstraction doesn't stop there. "A partner of the firm violated professional conduct today." It's the same idea, but now in highly conceptual language. If a writer has that idea in mind, he or she has to find some brute empirical see-hear-feel images and sounds to flesh it out for the screen play. Otherwise the director and actors will have to do the hallucinating and create their version of those words.

Representational Tracking
Translating back down the levels of thought from high abstractions to specific details is just as important as generalizing up the levels of mind. In fact, this flexibility of consciousness in moving up and down is one of the prerequisites of genius.

We have a tool, a linguistic tool, for translating great ideas at the higher or meta-levels of awareness back down so as to write the screen play in specific detail. We call it *Representational Tracking*. It means testing words to see if we can track them directly onto our movie screen or not.

This neuro-linguistic tool gives us the ability to reduce conceptual fog that abstract terms and language creates. The tool is a set of indexing questions. We use these *indexing* questions to find out the details so that we can make a Movie out of them. The questions allow us to explore the structure of an experience and to film that experience with precision. We use these questions to *index the specifics* of any statement so that we can then track over from the words and represent them in see-hear-feel terms on the screen of our mind.

Indexing questions search for specificity and details. Journalists have long recognized these questions as powerful for gathering high quality information without all the rigamarole. They ask who, when, where, what, how, which, and why questions. When we run our brains in this way, we can easily create internal Movies.

To create our mental Movies we track the information that words carry by *decoding the sensory information* in them. That then allows us to representationally track the sensory information onto the Movie in the theater of our mind. Conversely, when we question the words and language due to conceptual fog, we index specifics to find out how the screen play should look, sound, and feel like. Sometimes when we challenge the conceptual fog, it all vanishes. Poof! These questions have the effect of pulling the language narratives apart because the screen play was not well-formed. The story didn't cast a legitimate spell. So the questions de-hypnotize. They deframe. They cut and clip apart the old Movie scenarios. They stop those B-rated Movies in their tracks. Why? Because the Movies do not make sense. They are not well-structured or well-formed.

Who was the partner that violated the rules of professional conduct?
>What did Mr. Thompson do?
>How did he act like a fool?
>In what way did he show his anger?
>How do you know that he was upset?
>How specifically did he leave the room?
>What did he say?

When we use the indexing questions we inquire about *the form of the Movie* in the mind of the speaker. The questions enable us to question and challenge the impoverished screen play. It opens our eyes as to how the Movie teaches someone to have his or her limitations. This causes the Movie to stop, to change, and/or to cease to exist as it was.

This is the stroke of genius in the NLP linguistic model (called the Meta-Model). We use words as glue to link things together and as the frame to create perspective and focus. In this way words cue us about *what* and *how* to represent in our Movies. When a person, leaves out so much information, generalizes ideas in too broad of categories, or alters the idea then we can't accurately film the Movie that the person is trying to communicate.

Questions about the poorly constructed cinema will either elicit the specific details or *un-glue* the old editing. The questions take the fluff and vagueness out of the old scripts. Was Mr. Thompson really "unprofessional?" Who says that being professional prohibits feeling strongly about something and saying so? As we unthaw the frozen actions in the "nominalizations" (verbs turned into nouns), we break up the frames that govern the Movie and we invite the movie-maker to recover valuable sensory-based information.

What did Mr. Thompson consider non-sense?

He thought spending an hour talking about the colors for the firm's logo should have been delegated especially when one of the receptionists had lost her husband in an automobile accident that day?

The movie "magic" often occurs within our minds-hearts-bodies-and-emotions in response to indexing questions. It occurs because we get more information. We get a fuller description and not just the fluff words of one person's evaluation. Perhaps we might write a different screen play. "Mr. Thompson was the only partner who had the decency to put people before egos and stood up for Linda at the meeting."

To *representationally track* from what people say to the theater of our mind all we have to do is ask questions about specificity. We essentially ask people construction questions.

> How do you know?
> What lets you draw this or that conclusion?
> How do you know to construct things or interpret things in this way?
> What do you see, hear, feel, say, etc.?

To answer, we have to rise up in our mind, step out of the actors role and look at the screen play. This invites us to step up into a director's perspective. We have to move to a new space, to a place where we can operate as the editor or director of the Mand to think about things from those points of view. We have to rise up to a place where we can run our own mental Movies and make clearer decisions. In this way we can un-glue the words that scripted limiting Movies and Movie states. And, of course, that opens up new space for writing or narrating an entirely new plot.

"Making Sense" at Higher Levels
In translating back down from higher abstractions, we index specifics. Conversely, when we move up the levels and make evaluative conclusions about things, we use language that's increasingly more abstract. In doing this, we leave the realm of the brute empirical facts.

This explains why abstract ideas do not easily lend themselves to literal see-hear-feel representations. It also explains why it is more difficult to make a Movie out of our ideas about social justice, responsibility, honor, etc. We can put these words into the sound track:

> "I'm talking about justice ... I'm talking about honoring the memory of those who have made this freedom possible!"

Yet in doing so, we still need some sensory references.

In the mind, as we move up the levels, we often get lost in the world of words, especially in abstract words. Sometimes we are fortunate or creative enough to relate an abstract idea to empirical image, sound, sensation and can then use that see-hear-feel item as a metaphor that stands for the abstraction. We do this regularly when we relate the concept of "justice" to an image of balancing scales. We may relate the idea of "liberty" or "freedom" to the Statute of Liberty.

Then our see-hear-feel Movie of Miss Liberty can metaphorically represent a conceptual understanding. Newspaper political cartoonists do this all the time. In the USA, the two major political parties are pictured and symbolized as an Elephant (Republicans) and a Donkey (Democrats). Once we have these images, then we can make a Movie of them fighting a duel with swords, being in the same bed with each other, one stopping a wheelbarrow of pork and the other pushing it, etc.

Symbolic representations as these give us a way to create mental Movies of higher level concepts. The classic story of Einstein imagining himself on the end of a bolt of lightning flying through the universe and playing ball with someone on another bolt illustrates one of the many creative thought experiments he used to "think" about relativity.

All of this now gives us a new understanding of the processes that we call "communication," "reading," "understanding," etc. These are movie making processes. We succeed in these areas when we can produce an internal Movie in the theater of our mind. When we can't, we feel confused or ignorant.

What does this mean for learning, for intelligence?
It means that the more skilled we become in using our Cinema Mind—the more we can know, comprehend, and create.

Refreshing Your Best Movies

While we film things and store our memories as part of our video-library, these old Movies can fade and deteriorate and even become lost. We can and do forget things. We can take courses of study and write elaborate notes and years later we can examine the notes and then for the life of us can't ever remember any of that. Mental Movies have to be used and viewed and reviewed to be kept fresh. Our memories fade as the sensory details of our pictures, sounds, sensations, etc. fade out on the screen of our mind. This is just part of the way our Cinema Mind works.

It is *not* true that we remember everything that we ever see, hear, feel, smell, or taste. That myth arose as a tentative conjecture by the studies that Penfield did in the 1950s as the field of the neuro-sciences began. Penfield was the researcher who opened the human brain and stimulated various parts of the cortex with an electrical probe and discovered that his patients were suddenly flooded with memories that seemed so real, so vivid that it was like being there again.

In the pop psychology and self-help fields many have continued to jump to the conclusion that "the unconscious mind knows it all, remembers everything." But that's not the case. As a bio-electrical-chemical system, our brain-body system of cells are in constant motion and transition and change. In fact, every seven years we get a whole new set of cells. So memory storage has to be active and alive to keep knowledge alive. This explains the importance of refresh our thoughts. That's why repetition is so important. Via repetition, we keep running the neuro-pathways and all the mystery that goes on at the cellular and molecular levels.

To really remember the Movies we've seen and enjoyed, we need to watch them again from time to time. So with the Movies in the theater of our mind. We need to refresh them from time to time—this helps to keep our Movies alive, vital, and updated. In fact, from the point of view of really becoming masterful in running your own brain, suppose you regularly refreshed your best Movies?

Refreshing Your Best Movies for Increased Vitality
1) Identify five favorite states.
> What are five of your most favorite mental and/or emotional states? It could be confidence, playfulness, laughter, challenge, etc. Pick five of your favorites.

2) Match Movies to states.
> What Movies elicit these states in you? Identify actual Movies that elicit the states in you or your own mental Movies of events, experiences, and situations that have or that could elicit these states in you.

3) Edit each Movie for maximum elicitation.
> Take one state and one Movie at a time. First step into it to see how well the Movie, as you now have it encoded, elicits that resourceful state for you. Then step back from the Movie and up into the editor's and director's role and update it so that it maximumly elicits that favorite state in you. Continue until just the thought of that mental Movie puts you into the state. Make sure you have it well anchored in as many sensory systems as you can.

Summary

- Our MovieMind works by representing sensory information to create an internal video record of what we have seen, heard, felt, smelled, etc.
- We even use this mind to use abstract words as the screen play that tells us how to encode the Movie and the qualities to edit into it.

Chapter End Notes

*1 This illustration comes from Orson Wells which we quoted in full in *Communication Magic* (2001).

Chapter 5

CINEMA PERSPECTIVES

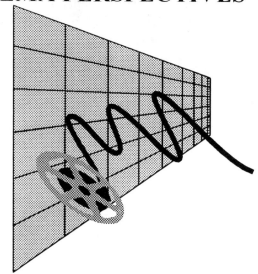

It's Your Point of View

"Okay, so we all have a Cinema Mind. So what?"

Actually there are many fascinating and magical things we can do with our mental Cinemas. As we take charge of our internal world, we can generate great Movies to make our life more alive and dynamic. One of the most spectacular is this: We can both *step in* and *out* of the Movies in our minds. We can take multiple perspectives to whatever is playing on the Cinema. This is the foundation for expanded knowledge and even for that exalted state that we call "wisdom."

The typical default viewing perspective of our Movies is from *within.* We see things from the eyes of being the actor. Normally we encode things from the inside because that's where we are when we first engage our senses of sight, sound, and sensation. Yet we don't always have to play the role of *the actor* in our Movies, we can step out.

We can step out to any position that a camera can film, an editor can invent, a director can imagine, or a producer can choose. We can view the Movie from directly in front, behind, to the right side, left side, from the crane position, from the projection booth, from a fish eye lens—the range of possibilities are enormous. We can view it from inside another person, from the point of view of an animal, the narrator, God, and even from another dimension.

Inside Out
The default perspective is always from *inside* the Movie and from out of our own eyes, ears, and skin. It's no mystery as to why this should be. After all, that's how we perceive things neurologically. We see out of our own eyes, hear out of our own ears, and feel from out of our own skin. There's really not much of a choice about this. It's a biological fact and constraint. It's also the way we learn to use our body as we grow up.

The idea of seeing things from *another person's point of view*, or feeling things as if from *inside the other's skin* is just that—an *idea.* It's not real. We have never *actually* stepped into another person. No body snatchers here. "Seeing things from another's point of view" is just a way of talking. We imagine what it would be like *if* we could. We entertain *the idea* of taking on the other's perspective, feelings, and frame of mind. We do it at the *conceptual* level, rather than a literal level. And yet we can do it so much and so well that as we entertain such thoughts and perspectives, we take on the feelings that are very similar to the other person's. Yet it is not *their* thoughts and feelings, it is still *our* thoughts and feelings inside *our* body. We have simply taken on the ideas that allow us to have similar feelings.

Stepping *into* and *out of* a Movie enables us to experience a wider and broader range of perspectives and understandings. This creates a flexibility of consciousness so that we never feel stuck in a particular role, scene, movie, or situation. Practically this means that we do *not* have to keep running old B-Rated Movies in our heads over and over and over. We can step out of those Movies. We can turn them off. We can erase them. We can update them, re-edit them.

Stepping out of our mental Movies also gives us the power to take on new perspectives that will increase our resourcefulness. This is another one of those intuitive things that we all seem to just know. Sometimes, in fact, we put it just that clearly.

> "You know, I think I just need a new perspective on this."
> "Yes, I can see your perspective but I'm wondering if you ever thought about that in this way ..."
> "If I could just get some distance to that problem, I know I could solve it. It just seems so close that it seems to close in on me."
> "In a hundred years, what difference will it make?"

Cinematic Play in your Mental Theater
1) Recall a film of an argument.
> Have you ever argued with another human being?
> Have you ever argued with someone and felt absolutely certain that you were right? Recall that event.

2) Play the film.
> Run the Movie of that event in whatever way you

remember it. Do so from beginning to end.

3) Change positions.

    Step into the other person's eyes and presence and see the arguing you and play the Movie from beginning to the end from this perspective.

4) Check effect.

    Did it make a difference? What did you learn? Do you now feel as certain as you did?

Cinematic Enrichment

As we view our thoughts as an internal Movie, we are able to apply all of the *cinematic features of a Movie* to the way we process information. The Movie metaphor for thinking and information processing translates our thoughts or operationalizes them to the sensory specifics of empirical reality, something that we can video-tape. The distinctive qualities of the video-tape corresponds to the cinematic features of our mental Movies. So when we step back from our Movie we are then able to frame it as close or far, bright or dim, in color or not, fuzzy or clear, loud or quiet, etc. This allows us to use the cinematic features to make multiple adjustments to our "thinking." That is, to the way we map our mental Movie.

We map the world using our internal Movie as young children and only later, as we mature, do we begin using more abstract symbols and notations. These make up a higher or meta-representation system and allows us to think and reason with more abstract symbols (e.g., language, mathematics, music, etc.).   With language we enter into the symbolic world of abstractions. When this happens, many people lose their awareness of their cinematic seeing and hearing. As they get lost in a world of words, sights and sounds fade. As they rise up to deal with things more abstractly, in terms of concepts rather than the see-hear-feel images, they lose awareness of their Movies.

This tends to be an occupational hazard of most advanced studies. Psychological tests going back into the middle of the nineteenth century discovered that the more college and university experience a person has, the less they can recall visually what they had on their plate for breakfast. When psychologist Galton considered that result, he concluded that the more intelligent we are, the less we visualize and conversely, the more we visualize, the less our intelligence. More recently another psychologist, Howard Gardner, has corrected that misunderstanding with his Multiple Intelligences model which includes visualization as one of the seven intelligences.

Yet university training, and even lots of reading, can move us out of the primary realm of our see-hear-feel images and into *the world of words*. As we then use words to *stand for* and *to represent* entire Movies of things, people, events and even more abstract things of the mind, classes, categories, and concepts, we become less conscious of our Movies.

Indeed, shifting from the more concrete thinking in empirical images to the more abstract and conceptual thinking describes one of the stages in cognitive development as noted by Piaget and others. Yet moving to conceptual thinking does not mean or imply that we cannot, or do not, see images any longer. It only means that we have supplemented our Movie with higher conceptual frames. And it can be a rush. No doubt about it. Watch and listen to a group of sophomores debating the philosophical questions of life. Abstract thinking enables us to transcend the empirical level thereby making it seem more primitive and infantile.

It is this marvelous ability to encode things symbolically that allows us to create increasingly abstract levels of linguistics and semantic meanings. This is our glory, especially when we don't get lost in the ozone and know how to bring our higher levels of conceptualization back down to our everyday Movies.

"Cut ... Let's Try Another Angle"

Have you ever been insulted or put-down or yelled at? Most of us have plenty of videos in our archives that would fit the category of *Insult Films*. Pull one of those out and let's play with it. Recall a time when someone was obnoxious or nasty to you or when a person raised his voice or she took you to task for some mistake that you made. Pull out a good juicy example of a scenario of insult.

> Has anyone ever in your entire life ever said something to you that was sarcastic, degrading, or unpleasant? From your archives of video features, pull out a memory.

As you do, notice how you think about it as your default setting. Are you there again? Are you *inside* the Movie receiving the insult and pretty much seeing what you saw then, hearing what you heard, and feeling what you felt? Just experience this briefly, noticing what it's like, what you feel. Good. Now stop.

Let's now do something mind-blowing. *Step outside* that Movie. Put the Movie up on the screen in your mind and take a seat out in the tenth row and ... oh yes, grab your popcorn or favorite snack, and just settle back in that comfortable chair to watch this B-rated Movie for the last time. As an observer of the film, you can now do some other pretty magical things. First, freeze frame the first picture of this film, turn it into a black-and-white snapshot ... and make sure that the Movie theater you're in is in color while the snapshot of the freeze-frame is black-and-white.

From the observer's point of view, let the Movie play and you be the movie critic. Watch it from the perspective of writing a review of the acting, the quality of the production, and whether you think it will win an Oscar or not. Cut out the laughter and just do it.

So what do you think? An award winning production? A pathetic film that won't even make it to the family reunion's funniest home videos?

Let's play it again, this time step into the Film and into the position of the person letting you have it with the insult or put-down. This may be a little more difficult role to imagine, but just for the fun of it, step into the body of the perpetrator of the insult, and look around using that person's eyes and ears. Then playing their role for a moment, watch that *other you* get the tongue lashing or whatever happened.

Step out of that role and let's take the perspective of someone who really loves you and cares about you. Put them into the background of the Movie and then step into that person's body. When you feel fully embodied in the one who loves you, watch the scenario play from that person's eyes. Notice what that's like. Be in that compassionate and caring perspective until it is all over and then from that role do whatever seems most natural and appropriate. For instance, you might feel the urge to go up to that other and give a loving embrace or high-fives.

All of these are, of course, just other perspectives, other points of view. With each new perspective, each new angle—*the Movie changes*. Perspective does that. Perspective colors the content of our Movie in new and different ways. Now see if you can remember how you had this *Insult Film* originally coded and get

that one back. If you can't, then try even harder. More often than
not, just the process of going through some other perspective
leaves a lasting influence on your mental videos. It's your own
internal Movie magic.

Editing your Insult Movie

The editing we've done so far is just *the editing of perspective.*
Yet we can edit it in so many more ways. This time let's explore
our Insult Movie in terms of its cinematic features.

1) Playfully Edit.

 As you do, let's curiously explore it from the perspective
of how you have coded the Video in the visual, auditory,
and kinesthetic channels. What are the qualities and
properties of your video? Use the list of cinematic
features that follows on the next page as a guide. Notice
what happens when you play around with editing your
cinema in various ways.

 How resourceful or unresourceful do you find your default
settings?

 If unresourceful, how would you like to change them?

2) Step back to examine the frames on this Movie.

 How have you framed this Movie in terms of attitude?
That is, what is your attitude *about* this Insult Movie?
What do you think about it, believe about it, expect,
understand, etc.?

 How resourceful or unresourceful are these frames?

 If unresourceful, what would be a more resourceful frame?

3) Step back one more level from the Movie.

 As you move to the Producer level in your mind about this
Movie, what are your purposes, motivations, and
intentions in producing this Movie?

 Do you need to update your intentions?

Do you need to update how to better fulfil the intentions?

4) Step back (or up) one more level.

> From the executive level of your mind, do you need this Insult Movie?
>
> If so, then how do you need to encode it so that it works to enhance your life?

5) Confirm, solidify, and future pace.

> As you alter your Movie, its default settings, and the frames at the higher levels of your mind, are you now satisfied with it? Would it now serve as a useful and enhancing reference?

Before we move on, here's one more thing to recognize and notice about your Cinema Mind. Did you notice *how* we called forth the video that we have been playing with? We did so by using an abstract word, "insult." This is not an empirical word. You cannot see "insult," you cannot hear it, feel it, smell it, or taste it. It doesn't exist at that level. "Insult" is a category term, a term that indicates a classification of ways of acting and speaking. We can see and hear "yelling," rolling the eyes, giving a finger, etc. But not "insult." Yet by using this more abstract term, we are able to access our video-library of films fitting that category. This is how we classify and store our audio-video archives—with evaluative terms.

Cinematography 101: Cinematic Features

The following offers many of the key distinctions that we use in editing the Movies in our MovieMind. These are sorted in terms of the basic sensory systems: visual, auditory, kinesthetic, and linguistic. To simplify things, we have included the olfactory sense of smell and the gustatory sense of taste under the kinesthetic.

The Visual Track of Pictures, Images and Movies:

Brightness:	Dull	—	Bright
Focus:	Fuzzy	—	Clear
Degree of Color:	Light/ Pastel	—	Bright/ Bold
Particular Color:	Disliked/ Liked		Favorite
Fact of Color:	Black-and-White —		Full Color Range
Size:	Small	—	Large
Distance:	Far	—	Close
Contrast			
Movement:	Still	—	Full of Action
Direction/Location:	Right	—	Left
	Above	—	Below
	Tilted	—	Straight on
Salience of Figure:	Foreground	—	Background
Frames: Snapshot	—	Movie	
	Still Picture	—	Moving Film
Number of Images:	Single	—	Multiple
Edges of Pictures:	Bordered —	Panoramic	
Shape / Form:	Normal, Fisheye, Flattened, etc.		
Horizontal & Vertical Perspectives: Ratio			
Perspective:	Associated	—	Dissociated
Actor Position —	Multiple Camera:		
	Editor, Director, Producer, etc.		
Dimensionality:	Flat 2-D image	—	3-D, holographic

The Auditory Sound Track of Sounds, Noise, Music, and Words

Content:	What is said		
Pitch:	Low	—	High
Location of Sounds:	Front / Back	—	Panoramic
	Up / Down	—	Single Source
Nature of Sounds:	Continuous	—	Interrupted, On-and-Off
Tone Quality:	Pleasant	—	Unpleasant
Tone Style:	Accent		
Number of Sources:	One	—	Many
Perspective:	Associated	—	Dissociated
Tempo:			
Inflection:	What inflection used?		
Volume:	Low	—	High
Rhythm:	Noise (no rhythm) —		Presence of Rhythm
Duration:	On-and-off	—	Endures
Distance:	Close	—	Far
Clarity:	Vague, Fuzzy	—	Crystal Clear
	Unintelligible	—	Intelligibility

Whose Voice:	Identification of Voice:	Self, Real, Imagined, Invented
Music: What Music?		
Melody:		

The Linguistic Sound Track of Words and Language:

Location of Words:	Above / Below;	—	Single source Multiple
	As Sound Track	—	As Visual Images
Level:	Sensory Based	—	Evaluative
	Simple, Empirical	—	Complex
Source:	From Self	—	From Others

The Kinesthetic Track of Sensations and Feelings:

What sensations:	Warmth, Movement, Pressure, etc.		
Pressure:	Light	—	Intense, Heavy
Location:	Where on Body or in Body?		
Extent of sensation:	Local	—	Pervasive
Moisture:	A Little	—	A Lot
Shape:	Scattered, pin-point, round, up-and-down, etc.		
Texture:	Rough	—	Smooth
Temperature:	Cold	Warm	Hot
Movement:	Kind and Nature	—	
Duration:	Momentary		Repeating Continuous
Intensity:	Light	—	High
Frequency:	Timing, pattern	—	
Rhythm:	—		—
Smells:	—		—
Tastes:	Sour / Sweet	Bitter / Salty	

Cinematic Exercises

It's time to play. Take time to explore and play with the following exercises as a way to become more fully acquainted with the cinemas of your mind. These exercises are designed to empower you to truly "run your own brain" as you become the editor, director, producer, and executive CEO of the Movies that play in your brain. If you're serious about mastering your own mind, do not skip this.

Editing Your Screenplay from Stress to Serenity

1) Identify a serenity Movie.

> Have you ever been in a state of calm peacefulness? Have you ever experienced a get-away from life's everyday hassles and stresses where you just relaxed fully and completely?

> Scan through your mind until you identify the place, situation, or experience that allowed you to experience such serenity and go there, turn on that video again and step into the Movie to re-experience it fully.

2) Test the power and usefulness of your serenity Movie.

> While still inside your serenity Movie, think about some of the current challenges, difficulties, stresses, and pressures that you face in your everyday life.

> How well do the serenity feelings hold when you invite the stress thoughts into that Movie? Gauge on a 0 to 10 scale.

3) Update the production of your serenity Movie.

> Rise up in your mind to the level of editor and director and check out the script that occurs when you think about life's everyday stresses. Notice the voice, the tone, the volume, the words, etc.

> Do you need to update the sound track and screen play of the script that occurs when you think about the stressors? If so, then do that. Eliminate every term, word, or phrase that interrupts the calm serenity and replace it with a more neutral or positive term. Add a soothing voice that's strong, confident, and resilient.

> What else do you need to re-edit so that while facing life's everyday stresses, demands, and pressures, you can operate from a serene center?

4) Quality control the end result and future pace.

> Would you like to take this into all of your tomorrows?

Will you?

Are you fully aligned with this?

Listen to Them Talk!

All over the world people are doing these kinds of things inside their minds as they edit their mental Movies. It's typically outside-of-awareness, but it happens none-the-less. Not only that, they are also announcing what they are doing. All we have to do is to listen to them talk. How? *Listen to talk* as if it were *screen play language.* Yes, it's a weird experience, yet it will cue you as to what they are doing in their brains.

"I can't *see* it that way."

"If I could only *get above it* all, then things would be fine."

"One of these days, I know that I'll *look back* on this and laugh."

"I just need to get some *distance* from it all. It's too close."

Stepping Out

The idea and feeling of *stepping out* of first position as actor in our Movies creates a weird and wonderful experience. Informationally, we are able to add new and different thoughts and perspectives to our understanding of things and this increases the richness of our mind. Emotionally, we correspondingly feel some new and different emotions as we step out. First of all, we feel the emotions that correspond to the additional points of view and perspectives. This enriches our emotional intelligence of the situation. Yet in our mental-and-emotional experience we also sense something else, a sense of transcendence. After all, in *stepping out* we transcend our perspective, our body, and ourselves if we do so only "in our mind."

In the *stepping out* of first position, we take a different perspective to ourselves. We can imagine thinking and feeling as another person in the Movie. If we *step into* the receiver of our words and actions, it creates for us an empathetic point of view. It allows us to understand, at least to some extent, what the other experiences.

If we *step into* the narrator's point of view, the editor's, the director's, the audience's, the God point of view, a point of view from the future or one from the past—we are able to add these awarenesses to our own. In fact, by stepping out of the actor's perspective, we can *step into* any other mind-body *state.* Then, we can take on the thoughts-and-feelings of that state.

Stepping out itself feels weird to the extent that we do not extend ourselves and take on other points of view. At first we may not know how to think or feel and so feel as if we are spacing out, or in a trance, or dis-embodied. If we step out because the actor's position is very painful, traumatic, and even unacceptable, we may not have a target state to step into ... and so we step into, as it were, an emptiness. So that's what we feel, empty, emotionless, outside of ourselves, numb. Of course, those are not *un-emotions*, but emotions also, or perhaps more accurately, judgments and evaluations, meta-feelings (meta-states).

> [In psychiatric terms, this is often called "dissociation." We dis-associate from our normal and typical thoughts and feelings ... due to the unpleasantness or pain of such. If we do this around our sense of identity, we create a dissociative identity disordering.]

Stepping out and into really positive states and states that seem higher, more valuable, more profound, more spiritual—gives us the sense of "transcendence." That is, rising above ourselves, and *transcending* everyday reality for some higher reality. This is what most people feel when they experience what we call the "spiritual" emotions: love, joy, ecstasy, compassion, unity, oneness, a higher purpose, a calling, etc.

Stepping out of our first position as actors in our Movies is the foundation and basis of all of the higher states of mind-and-emotion that we can attain. Especially valuable is *stepping into* the Editor's role, the Director's role, and the Producer's role as we will explore in the coming chapters.

Cinematic Perspectives

First Position: Actor Participant.

> When we are inside the Movie, we are in *the actor's position* and so experience the *actor's perspective*. We see, hear, and feel as if experiencing the actions and the drama. This is the normal default setting for our Movies and the one most of us experience most vividly and powerfully.

Second Position: Empathetic, Another Actor.

> When we shift to another person's role inside the Movie, we take the role of another actor, one that we have to imagine what that would be like. In that sense, we create that perspective inside our mind *about* it. Typically, this position will not be as immediate or vivid. This is the perspective of sympathy and empathy.

Third Position: Observer, Learner.

> This is the position that we take when we step aside from the Movie and just observe it. This is the spectator's point of view. This is the point of view from the audience or from a balcony. It's a more neutral position, a more objective one.

Fourth Position: Editor.

> We use this one for the editor's perspective. Here we step outside the Movie and take the point of view of looking at

it from the perspective of how the Movie or film is structured or framed.   Here we can bring all of our editorial skills and movie magic to the Movie.

Fifth Position: Director.

Beyond the role of editor is that of *director*.   From this point of view we look at the cinema in terms of what we are directing and managing.   The director's perspective manages what the editor does and the camera positions. The director gives directions to the actors with regard to how to play the role and to give the part the attitude that the screen play calls for.

Sixth Position: Producer or Executive.

One step further out from the director is that of the *producer and executive* role.   In this perspective, we see things from an even broader point of view —from the perspective of what we are producing, the over-all effect that it has, it's quality and usefulness.

Seventh Position: All Other Positions.

We use this position to refer to all other perspectives, especially conceptual points of view: from the past, future, an all-knowing narrative, an angel, etc.

Summary

- Every film contains within it a perspective. Most Movies have many perspectives.   These perspectives enable us to encode the Cinemas of our mind with multiple understandings.
- While we typically experience our Movies from *within* as an actor playing out our role, we can *step out* of that role and take on many others.   This expands our choices and enriches our inner world. The more flexibility we have in doing this, the greater and richer our perspective on things.

- In this chapter we explored three other videos from our archives: an Insult Film, a Stress Movie, and a Serenity Cinema.
- Learning to control when you are *in* and *out* of the Movie gives us a profound and pervasive way to improve the quality of our lives.

Chapter 6

MOVIE STATES

This Movie Always Makes Me Feel X...

Typically when we go out to a movie or get a movie at a video store, we run *a feeling check.* We check to see what we *feel* like seeing. Why do we do such a thing? We do so because we know there's a relationship between the movies we watch and the emotions that follow.

How about a horror movie? A real white-knuckle thriller that will keep you on the edge of your seat looking over your shoulder?

How about an adventure movie? A cliff-hanger adventure movie that never lets up with the hero and heroian always on the verge of disaster?

What about a comedy? Slap-stick or more subtle?

And of course there is Romance, Drama, Children, Educational, Documentary, Game Shows, Porno, Crime, etc.

What do you want to see?
What do you want to feel?

Not infrequently, we don't feel "in the mood" to see a particular kind of movie. We don't want to have to deal with those emotions.

So it is with the Movies in our minds. They trigger, stimulate, evoke, provoke, and excite *emotions*, emotional states.

Movies and Emotions
- What creates our mind-body *states?* That is, our mental states and our emotional states.
- Where do they come from?

They come from our mental Movies—from our MovieMind.
Play a horror Movie in your mind and guess what feeling states you will conjure up? The same goes for a Movie full of rage and anger, joy and playfulness, a comedy, drama, meta-drama, etc. The Movies we play on the theater of our minds cue our bodies about how to feel and what to do.

Our mental Movies are not neutral.
There's a price to pay for every Cinema you create and entertain in your mind. And you will pay the price for admittance to that audio-video experience in terms of your kinesthetic sensations or feelings, your emotions, your health and well-being, your sanity and adjustment to reality, and your responses. What price are you paying for the Movies playing in your mind?

The relationship between what goes on in our mind in terms of the cinematic features and our mind-body states of consciousness describes a fundamental principle about our mind-body functioning. This is why we have to take charge of what we are watching if we want to "run our own brain" and control our own *states.*

Why is this?

Because our mind-body-emotion *states* are functions of the Movies we play in our Cinema Mind.

"Thinking" starts out as *the re-presentation* (presenting again) of the sensory information that we have experienced in the world. But it doesn't end there. In addition to what we encode from our sense receptors, we say words about our representations. We create a narrative account of what it means. This gives us higher or meta-representation sense of things. In addition to the Movie, there is the sound track of words as well as the words that we can lay over the film to signal scenes, times, and meanings.

Every representation affects us, the frames invite us to experience the Movie in a certain way and so evoke mind-body-emotion states. Even when the frame of the Movie is that of "just watching," witnessing, and observing, we do not experience things without some emotion or physiological state. The emotion may be mild, calm, relaxing, and hardly noticeable. Yet we are breathing, moving, experiencing some posture. We are not dis-embodied. Even when we feel "numb," we are still feeling a feeling, even if it is a meta-feeling.

Every sensory-rich Movie that we construct on the screen of our mind affects us neurologically and so influences our state of "mind," "emotion," and "body." While we so readily use these terms as if they were separate elements, they are not. Our language tricks us here. *Mind-body-emotion all work together as a system.* By the way, this is the reason I hyphenate these words. The hyphen reconnects the system.

Every thought and representation that we encode on the Cinema of our mind and frame evokes mind-body *states.* We cannot dismiss or discount our internal Movies as innocent, harmless, or irrelevant. They are not. *States*, as in neuro-linguistic and neuro-semantic states, make up the very heart of all our experiences. When we process information from reading, listening, or communicating, we go into states. And while our physiology and neurology certainly contributes to these states, it is our internal Cinemas that primarily govern the quality and kind of our states.

This is why it is so important to learn how to "run our own brain." The Movies that we run in our brains, and the ways that we frame those Movies, determines our experiences, self, skills, destiny, relationships, health, etc.

Phil's emotions over his *Inadequacy Movie* (Chapter 1) conjured up tremendous emotions of inadequacy. Movies create and evoke these emotions. In Terri's case, she had a *Hurt Movie* playing, yet she was far less conscious of it because she had always tried to make the Movie go away by rejecting it. Yet it continued to play ... creating emotions she hated and didn't want and so she created a false persona.

Cinematographical Emotions
We feel what we feel because of the Movies playing in the theater of our minds.

As we map out various screen plays and movie scripts, so we represent them. As we create the appropriate audio-visual tracks of the Movies along with the sound track with the words that we use to narrate the meaning of the Movie—so we go into state.

This explains the rhyme and reason of our emotional states. Yet we are mostly unconscious of our Movies. What are we consciously aware of ? Our emotions. Our somatic bodily sensations, feelings, responses, and what our motor programs are urging us to do. That's what we're aware of. Our consciousness goes to the *result* of our internal computations, map-making, framing, and meaning-making not to the processes. Our attention goes to what our body is experiencing as we register the evaluative impact of the internal Movie with our sense of the external world.

That's why *emotions*, emotional urges (drives, needs), and behaviors are much easier to notice and focus on than the internal processes that create them. Yet our emotions result as symptoms of our internal processing. That's why trying to change an emotion *directly* typically seems next to impossible. "Commanding" our emotions, for the most part, is not an effective intervention.

To change our emotions, and all of the bodily processes involved in an emotional state, we have to go higher. We have to retrace our steps back to the mental Movie that encodes our mapping and the frames of our Cinema. Transformation of our state occurs when we change the Movie—when we change the screen play, the script, how it is edited, or how it is framed. Play a different Movie and different states will emerge.

What are Your Cinematic Emotions?
If playing inside your Cinema Mind is a film full of blame, accusations, counter-accusations, attacks on people's motives, intelligence, etc., then you'll see the world in those terms, and you will feel accordingly. What will you feel? You will feel defensive, blamed, accused, insulted, put-down, etc. Or, if you play the role of the Blamer in the Movie, you might feel insecure and defensive and so you take the offensive and blame, accuse, feel self-righteous, arrogant, self-important, etc.

If you play the B-rated Movie, *"I'll Never Amount to Anything,"* you'll probably feel worthless, hopeless, and helpless. You'll probably experience feelings of being a victim, not having a fair chance, and doomed to inadequacy.

I know what people who live in fear, anxiety, dread, and terror watch on the theater of their minds. They do *not* watch Movies of being resourceful, playful, loving, etc. No, they watch Horror Movies! Their fear, anxiety, dread, and terror make perfect sense.

From Movie to Meaning

How does "meaning" enter into our mental Cinemas? What is the relationship between our sensory Movies and the phenomenon of meaning?

Meaning at the first level of representation arises from what we have associated. This creates *associative meaning*. We do this by linking things together. On the screen of our mind we link an event together with a way of thinking or feeling. In this way, we can associate the strangest things together. These become the frames of our mental Movie. As we produce or film things in this way, so it becomes to us.

When we step into the first position and we are the actor of the Movie, things take on the *meanings* according to how we link the events together. At this level, the sequence of events creates the "meaning." From inside the Movie we see-hear-and-feel a sequence of events: first event A happens, then event B, then event C. This creates our sense of the meaning of the Movie. We interpret the Movie according to how the associations are sequenced. We interpret it according to where the Movie takes us.

Suppose we go into a dark haunted house and that evokes fear.

We then add some suspenseful music and then an attack by an intruder. What does all of this "mean?" We will undoubtedly interpret the darkness, music and the attack in terms of threat, danger, and fear. Simple linkage. We could have just as well linked other things to the darkness, suspenseful music, and attack—adventure, challenge, and curiosity. It could mean exploration, love, arousal, anger, joy, playfulness, etc. Watching some Pink Panther and old Charlie Chaplin movies with all those qualities elicits laughter.

At the level of the Movie's actions, we experience things from *inside* the Movie as we move from event to event. We enter into a strictly Stimulus—>Response world. It's a world where we see one thing, and then another. From this we conclude that the first *triggers* the latter. We reason the first *equals* the second. Linguistically this will show up in the screen play in the language of cause-effect and equivalence statements. The writer has written,

> "And the dark basement *causes* Sue to feel afraid. That's because it *is* a scary place."

Perhaps we have a Movie in our mind of being yelled at as a kid by dad every time we made even the simplest of mistakes. When he yelled, we felt afraid. Then, over time we came to use that Movie not merely for recoding the sequence of events, we use it for a different purpose. We might conclude, for instance, that "dad" is typical of all "people in authority" and so use that Movie to think about the class of authority figures. Now we have a Movie ready for how to make sense of, understand, and map how to respond to any authority figure we meet today. Or we could take the Movie of "yelling" and use "yelling" to be our way to think about the entire class of "humiliation," "put down," "controlled," or whatever category we create.

It is in this way that we begin to refer to, or reference, our history of memories of previous references and use them for abstract reasoning. This creates all of our *frame-of-reference meanings* that make up the Matrix of our mind. These higher level meanings show up in our Movies as the frames. It's the meaning frames that we use to interpret things.

Emotional Intelligence

- How do you feel?
- What are your habitual states?
- When do you feel particularly resourceful, or unresourceful?
- Are there any "buttons" that people can push to get you riled up?

Behind each of these emotional responses and patterns *there is a Movie.* Some may only flash across the screen of your consciousness for a moment (the zip file phenomenon), but it is there. This is the primary source for all of our emotions. When you know this and have developed the habit of stepping back to examine the features playing in the theater of your mind, you'll develop an intelligence about your emotions that will give you the key to mastery—mastery of self, of your emotions, of your life.

Add Pleasant Emotions

It's not infrequent in life that we find ourselves in a situation where we are in conflict with someone, struggling with a task or project, or just feeling stuck. Typically when this happens we become aware of things as not right, that something is wrong. In fact, we become painfully aware of this. It feels bad and so we film that experience. And because, at the director's level of mind, we don't want to feel bad, or to have this experience, we forbid it. We issue a directive that orders that emotion or experience off the set. "Out of here!" we thunder. We may even send security to escort the emotion or the experience out. In this way, we taboo our emotions as "bad." Yet does the mere forbidding of the experience or of our awareness of the experience make it go away? No.

The experience of feeling stuck, struggling, in conflict, challenged, etc., is one thing. Actually, it is just a problem to solve. But then we go and add unpleasant emotions to it. Of course, doing so is extra. We don't have to do that. The experience doesn't have to be experienced as negative. Actually, choosing to *feel bad about it is extra.* We could feel neutral or matter-of-fact, or better, we could feel curious, motivated, challenged, determined, resilient, persistent or any of a hundred more positive states. We could even add humor, fun, playfulness, and thrill to it.

Why do we add unpleasant feelings and feel bad about it? You've got it— because we play certain Movies at those times. We play various Movie clips: the Blues, the Down-and-Out, This Always Happens to Me, It's a Crappy Life, etc.

How could we add pleasant feelings? You've got it—by playing a different set of Movies. We could play our personalized version of the "Rocky" movies and get our own "eye of the tiger." We could play "The Sound of Music" and climb the mountain before us to a new life.

But why feel good when "bad" things or frustrating things are happening? Won't the Mind Police come after us? Mostly we add pleasant feelings because we become more resourceful when we feel good. We are easier to live with, more creative, we have more access to our highest values and visions, we are able to pull off miracles. Plus, it feels good.

Phil's Inadequacy Dragon Movie

Phil treated the thoughts and feelings of inadequacy as a dragon, as something bad and wrong and unacceptable. The Movie he had in his head was mostly a home video of his father and mother saying insulting things. "Why can't you be more like your older brother? What's wrong with you? You'll never make it!" It wasn't a two-hour epic, his Movie lasted only a couple of seconds. And he hated it.

Phil, I want you to put that Movie up on the screen of your mind and sit back and help me to peer inside.   So, just sit back in that chair ... and, what's your favorite snack to eat when you're watching a Movie? Chips and dip? Well, here's some imaginary chips and dip... just take them and I want you to watch this really stupid and mindless Movie for the last time. Good. Now as you do, really look at it ... and by the way, how old is that *you* in that Movie?

>   Oh, I don't know, maybe eight ... yes, eight or nine, not more than ten years old.

Really? My God, Phil, I thought we were talking about a Movie of an Inadequate Adult! You mean this "Dragon" is about an eight-year old *inadequate boy?* My God, man, what did you expect of yourself at eight?

>   (Laughing) That is ridiculous, isn't it? I never thought of it like that.

Well, look ... really look at that young kid. Look at that silly face and all of his boyish immaturity and what he wore... You'd never be caught dead wearing *those* clothes again, would you?

>   No, of course not.

Good. I thought we were going to really have a problem here. And notice where the voice of the judgment sound track in this Movie comes from ... that's right... and notice if it's your mother's voice or your father's. And feel free to begin to edit this Movie so that you can turn down the volume so you can barely hear it, or fade all of the colors out until it's an old fashion bland grey ... and you can add in music in the background that helps you to stay focused as you watch it.

Because as an adult you have so many more skills, so much more knowledge, and experience ... and you can take those competencies and when you're ready you can see something fabulous in this Movie ... you can see the adult you with all those competent resources, enter into that Movie as a mentor to that eight-year old boy you and speak to that younger you...

Stepping In and Out of Emotions

It's funny about some of the habits that some people develop and maintain. There are lots of people who always *step into their worst Movies* and take the actor's role as an active participant. Of course, this inevitably conjures up the worst emotions. Then, to make things even worse, they always *step out when they play their most wonderful and inspiring Movies.* They step out to observe and witness them as a non-participant. Of course, that leaves them deprived of filling up their "Feeling Good" bank account.

These people have it all turned around.
The best way to move through life and the best way to master your own Cinema Mind is to do the opposite. Whenever you film or recall a negative, unresourceful, and unpleasant Movie—*step out.* Just observe it. Learn from it. Use it as feedback and stay out of it. Wasn't once enough? Or, is there some particular thrill you get from feeling bad?

This is especially true when something doesn't go well, when a significant investment of time, money, mind, and heart is lost, when someone takes you on to play the Blame Game with, even when you go into self-criticism. *Step out!* Rise up in your mind to a level that gives you some distance so that instead of being inside the Movie, you can learn from it and see it from more useful frames.

Whenever you film a pleasant experience or recall having a great time or anticipate a marvelous one to yet happen—*step into it!* Be there. Amplify all your pictures, sounds, and sensations and invite your whole inner world to become *Sensorama Land.*

Why not? When we feel good we act more resourcefully and produce higher quality responses. This is especially true for making love, experiencing an exquisite pleasure, having fun with friends, achieving an important goal, or standing in awe and appreciation of the wonder and mystery of life. These are the kinds of emotions to treasure and "count" (rather than discount) and use to build up your resourcefulness.

Summary

- We feel, respond, and act the way we do because of the Movies playing in the theater of our mind. As we play adventure, comedy, documentaries, dramas, melo-dramas, tragedies, etc., so we set the feel and attitude of our lives.
- The feelings we experience spring from the roles we play and the script and plot in the screenplay.

Chapter 7

THE LEVELS OF CINEMATIC PRODUCTION

It Takes a Hierarchy to Make a Movie

If our mind is like a Cinema in the way we record our experiences and re-present information as an internal film, then the cinema metaphor for thought, emotion, and experience is also suggestive about *the levels* involved in producing a Movie. Obviously, to create a Movie we have to have *a film* on which to record things and actors on a stage carrying out some kind of plot or screen play. At the primary level, we need to fill up the screen with people doing things as they talk and feel and engage in various activities. We have people following a screen play of some sort and someone recording it.

So with the mind. We are always recording or representing something. There's always something *on* our minds. If we could peek into the theater of each other's minds, we would see people and things and activities and talk— the video-recorder is picking up the things that are happening. This theater is our "place for seeing" (our "theater").

But then we can back up and notice where *the cameras* are stationed and what they are focusing on. We can back up and notice how *the director* is giving instructions to pan wide, zoom in, re-do a scene, cut and print, etc. We might notice the director giving instructions to *the editors* about what editorial qualities to add to the final film to give it the qualities he or she wants.

And if we backed up a little further and took in a larger time span, we might notice *the producer* conferring with the director about what the studio wants. He might bring up some political or cultural concerns to be addressed.

This description identifies different *levels of influences* that go into the production of a film. So it is with the human mind-emotion-body system. There are also levels of awareness and representation that go into how we construct the Cinemas that we entertain in our minds.

It Takes a Hierarchy to Make a Movie
When we watch a Movie, we do *not* see all of the players. We do not see the directors, editors, camera people, etc. All of the things that went into the background to create that Movie are *not* inside the Movie. Sometimes a Movie will include various "take outs," and bloopers at the end of the Movie or even include a piece of "Movie magic" to explain how they made the Movie. We get a cue about all the others who created a Movie when we see the

credits at the end.

A similar thing occurs with regard to what's on "the screen of our mind." Other facets of our mind-body-emotion system have played a role in what we see and hear in consciousness. In addition to the many facets of our "unconscious cognitive" processing that we cannot even become aware of, there are also numerous outside-of-conscious awareness facets of mind that we can bring into consciousness. These are the higher levels of our mind.

Running with the cinema metaphor, this allows us to identify numerous cinematic levels.

Cinematic Levels
1) Representational Level
> What are you representing in your mind?
> What things are playing out on the screen of your consciousness?

This level describes *what* we see, hear, feel, etc. as our internal Movie plays. Typically we are *inside* the Movie and experiencing things as an actor or player in our thoughts.

2) Editorial Level
> How do you encode what you are representing?
> What kind of a film or Movie is playing? What is its quality?

This level describes *how* we structure, encode, and frame our Movie. From the editorial position, we decide where we put the camera and what perspective we use (the perceptual positions). From this level we edit the Movie with certain cinematic features.

3) Director Level

> What is our immediate intention and objective in filming or playing this particular Movie?
>
> What is the attitude or feel of this Movie?

At this level we direct ourselves and others as players inside the Movie. We give the actors their motivations and intentions and we establish the general attitude and disposition to be conveyed. We also direct the editor in the editing.

4) Producer and/or Executive Level

> What are our higher objectives and intentions in this production?
>
> How does this Movie fit into the overall cinematic productions that we've created?

Figure 7:1
Meta-Levels of
Internal Production

```
          ------------------- Director and/or Executive ---------------
        /                                                        \

      ----- Editor --------        and        ------- Camera Persons ------
     /                  \                    /                         \


                       THE MOVIE
                  Playing on the Screen of the Mind
```

At this higher level, we establish and operate from the value and identify frames that we have meta-stated into existence. At these levels we are focused on what we are producing and our sense of mission and destiny. Here we have a more mindful sense of having choice about the decisions we make that influence everything below it: producing, directing, editing, and experiencing.

Levels Inside the Embarrassment Film

Let's review the Movie we called forth from our archives of videos about some embarrassing moment at work, school, or with friends and notice the default settings we use in framing and formatting this Movie. This takes us to what we call *the cinematic distinctions.* We can notice if we portray the Movie encoded as still pictures or moving, black-and-white or in color, close or far, etc. This moves us to *the editor's perspective* of our mental Movies. As an editor, what have we put in the foreground? In the background? What perspective have we used in viewing the Movie? How dim or bright? From above or below? From the back or front?

Here we can use all of the techniques that any editor uses in producing a cinematic effect, multiple images, transparency, speeding up the film, slowing it down, etc. We can even use various "movie magic" tricks to create various visual and auditory effects.

When we move back from direct editing of the mental Movie in our mind, we move back (or up) to *the director's role.* Here we are not so concerned with the particular cinematic features, but with the attitude, intent, design, and focus that we want to convey through the Movie. By way of comparison, consider what a director does in directing the making of a film. While the director may ask the camera people to zoom in or out, to fade out with a fog coming in, etc., the director mostly asks the actors to play their parts with more or less flare, boldness, anger, fear, etc. The director may ask for more or less eye contact, speed of voice, or forcefulness of expression. In this he or she directs the *qualities* that texture the film in a certain way. This corresponds to the higher frames of mind that make up our *attitudes*—the attitudes that seep into our mental Movies.

When we take yet another step back or up, we move to the position of *the producer.* With each step there's a paradox. The actors in the Movies are a lot more involved than the camera people and editors, who are more involved than the director, who is more involved than the producer ... yet the producer has more long-term and pervasive influence than the director, who has more influence than the editor and camera people, than the actors. "Control" moves down the levels to the actors who just play the parts.

This means that ultimately, how we experience a film in our mental theater depends on the nature of the film, on what happens, and how we view it. It depends on how it is produced, directed, and edited.

Mystery Theater 3000 provides a great illustration. Here, in a futuristic theater aboard a space ship zooming through the galaxy, there is a human and two robots watching old B-rated Movies. Frequently of old sci-fi films of Godzilla, wolfman, and the like. But the B-rated Movies *feel* different in this context. They are more like comedies than scientific dramas or horror pictures. What causes this? The larger context. In *Mystery Theater 3000* we see the back of the human's head and the outline of the robots and they won't shut up with all of their snide remarks about the old films. They invite us into a state of ludicrous silliness about the old Movies and about themselves. We laugh at the old Movie and at them.

Terri's Hurt Movie

As I explored Terri's *Hurt Movie* with her, it became clear about the hurt that was eating her up. Her mother had rejected her when she was a child of three because she was a girl and not a boy. She was the next to the youngest after five boys in a rural farm family and for whatever reason, her mother could not or would not accept her. And while she never came out and said this, her thoughts and emotions spoke in a thousand little hints that were always tinged with sarcasm.

This *Rejection Movie* then began a motif theme in Terri's mind-body-emotion system. It was the proto-type for choosing men in her life—men who always seemed to somehow have a hatred of women and who only wanted to use women, and display them as "trophies" but never love them for who they were. Two divorces later, Terri now hated the "M" (marriage) word. She knew what "men" were like and what they wanted. It was in this way that her Movie kept evolving, taking on new dimensions, adding new lines to the screen play and being confirmed by real life experiences.

Yet it was just a Movie. It was just a Movie in her mind ... that she would not welcome in because "welcoming" it in *meant* to her to condone it and approve it. She was also *afraid* of it. *Afraid* that the Movie spoke the ultimate truth about her value and worth as a human being. Intellectually she knew better, but that "intellectual" Movie was just an academic documentary that didn't stand a chance against the Horror Movie that would not go away.

At the first level of that Movie, she was the key actress who was the hated and despised one that had no right to be there. When she stepped back from that, she *hated* that message and those feelings, but also *feared* that it was true. Back at the director's role she knew better and knew that no one should be so treated. Yet she had no replacement Movie of innate and unconditional value and worth or a new script to play a new screen play of dignity, value, openness. Whenever she would get a bit of that, she'd step back into the role of the hated and despised one. It was a vicious cycle.

The dragon first had to be slain. The dragon of thinking that she was worthless and didn't deserve to "be" which she had confirmed again and again ... would not let a new screenplay.

Levels of "Action" in our Cinematic Productions

Even our experience of what we do, our "actions" means something different at every level of our Movies. Consider the internal cinema that we run in our mind as we represent a new skill that we want to adopt.

At the primary level of the Movie, the new "actions" and activities are the things that we do *inside* our Movies as an actor. At this level we don't play the Movie for entertainment, we play it in order to step into it to use it as a model for what to do and how to feel. "Action" at this level describes what we are doing, saying, gesturing, behaving, etc. Here our actions are what we do as we play out the part—the role.

When we *step back* to the third position of the editor's role, we think *about* the film and from here may edit it a bit, add in this resource, zoom in on this or that idea or understanding, foreground an area of concern, etc. Our "actions" at this level are the actions of editing, of thinking about how to best encode and structure our informational video.

When we step into the fourth position of the director of the Movie, our actions are the actions of directing how we edit, the perspective we take, and the call to do it. From this level of mind, we say to the actor part of ourselves, "Lights, camera, *action!*" It is our ability to act at this level that leads us to *implement* our first level actions. At the director's level we decide, we make choices, we say yes and no to various options.

The same applies with the "actions" we take in the fifth and sixth positions. When we act as *producer* and *chief executive* of our Movies, we act to set policy, decide on how we want the instruction video to be directed, establish agenda, motivation, reason, and tie it all into our reason for living. All of these are very different kinds of "actions" —and yet they are all vital to the overall cinema.

Minding the Levels of our Cinema Matrix
Movies not only have objects (translating the nouns of our language) moving about on the screen and doing things (which translates the verbs we use in our descriptions), but all of this occurs inside of frames.

This is how we think. We start with a *referent experience.* That is, something happens. So we record it. We film it into our minds. In doing this, we create an internal *represented reference*, that is, our sensory based internal Movie. This frees us from having to have the referent experience again. Now we can recall it or remember it. As we present it to ourselves again (re-presentation), we can experience it again. It's like showing the old family home videos of a vacation except we do it in our minds and can do it anywhere and at anytime.

Now a funny kind of thing happens when we keep running our old Movies inside our heads. After awhile, the old video becomes so much a part of our mental landscape, that as a Library of Reference, we start using it as a *frame-of-reference.* It's like what happened when Star Wars first came out and some people saw them again and again and again, sometimes twenty times, sometimes a hundred times. After awhile, the people, activities, actions, language, and references in *Star Wars* became their universe. It became the world they live in. They begin relating everything to Luke Skywalker and Darth Vader and the Millennial Fulcan, etc. It became their everyday reference system.

A similar thing happens to us in our mental and conceptual world. We all have a natural proclivity to default to *our experiences*, to the reference experiences we have had. Yet as we do, we transform them into our *frames of reference.* Yes, it's circular thinking. Yes, it is junko logic. Yet it is the way all of us naturally think until we learn better. We reason and judge experiences *on the basis of* our experiences, even when our experiences were crappy, painful, ugly, limited, impoverished, etc.

"It's a Crappy Life"
This is probably "best" seen in the lives of those who have the misfortune of getting parents who skipped out on Parenting 101. As they grow up, they get a whole lot of *experience* in life, experiencing the worst things: being unloved, unappreciated, abused, neglected, insulted, filled with stupid lies and deceptions, taken advantage of, manipulated, etc.

Then, with those *referent experiences* all they have are a whole library of B-rated Movies of people being ugly and stupid to each other. That's the world they've lived in. They know nothing else. It is their Universe and they use *that* to judge everything else, even

Movies of healthy relationships.

So when they see, meet, and experience normal people, healthy people, people raised to love themselves, to have their own voice and mind, to be centered and focused, to be caring and passionate —it doesn't seem real. They don't trust it. They may not even like it.

After all, they know "reality." They have a whole video-arcade in their head (and heart and body) that "proves" that that's a bunch of B.S. When someone treats them well, they wonder, "What's wrong?" When someone treats them with respect and dignity, they wonder what that person is up to. When someone holds them accountable for their actions, they feel "blamed" and attacked. It's all a strange world.

This is the double-bind and Catch-22 of most of our Movies. Our Movies are just the recorded films of whatever we so happened to experience. Yet we use them for our sense of "reality." This is what starts the trouble. We get used to the Movie Land of our mind and then jump to the unfounded conclusion that it is "real," that it is "reality."

It is not. It is only reveals a recording of what we have been through. And if we've been through crap... well, then we have an extensive video-library in our head of Crap-Land. It says nothing about what's normal, what's healthy, or what's possible. Just what we have watched and then mis-used as our frames of reference.

Frame World
The story doesn't end with that.

Not only do we get use to our *references* and then assume that they construct *the Story of Reality*—which, of course, we have on video and have available whenever we need it. So, it is with the habituating of our frames and frames of reference that they become our *frames of mind*. That is, we actually begin to *see* the world and perceive things in these ways.

This describes how we all learn to *structure or format* our "mind." We take references, transform them into frames of references, then frames of mind and before long we have the frameworks of what we call "personality." What makes up the matrices of our mind? The embedded frames upon frames around some event or experience.

Or, in terms of internal Movies, we film an event. We create an audio-visual record of some second-rate experience. Then we keep playing it over and over in the theater of our mind. Playing it over and over makes it familiar to us which, even though the film is second-rate, at least we feel comfortable with it—we know its plot, characters, world, emotions, actions, and script. With repetition and no new releases entering the theater, we then jump a logical level and conclude, "This is the way life is for me." In this way we frame it as "Real," and "Inevitable."

We create layers of states as we relate one state to itself or to another state. This means that as we run one Movie on the screen of our mind, we have enough "mind," or awareness, that we can step back to notice the Movie and run a Movie about that one.

This is the way of "mind." *Mind* reflects upon itself and thereby builds up layers of embedded frames (technically we call these "meta-states"). Prior to Meta-States, we called these higher level states by many other terms which in itself created confusion and falsely led psychologists to think that these different terms referred to different "things." They do not.

What we call "beliefs, values, identity, decisions, purpose, understandings, expectations, paradigms, knowledge, mission, intention," etc. are nominalized descriptions of mind acting and doing things such as believing, valuing, deciding, understanding, expecting, etc. These terms nominalized the actions.

By the way, a "nominalization" is the noun-ing of a verb which then makes the verb (the set of actions) sound like a thing or entity. In this way, "relating" becomes "Relationship." But nominalized verbs are not real "things" or "entities" at all. At best we might say that they are "things" of the mind. Yet we are the one who calls them into existence and we do so by *thinking* them into existence. They are "real" to that extent.

For example, what do you *believe* about becoming financially independent or wealthy? What's your frame of mind about that? Suppose you believe, "Rich people get that way by taking undo advantage of others in deceptive ways." Or, "Money is the root of all evil" (to mis-quote a Bible verse). If that's at the top of your mind, then you can imagine what will result when you play a Movie about how to build wealth, budget, sell, etc. The very same educational documentary playing in another person's mind will create a very different effect than in the mind of someone whose CEO thinks the whole think stinks.

As we move up "the levels" and layer thought upon thought, feeling upon feeling, physiology upon physiology and all of these in various combinations, we are simply *framing* the main Movie. Doing this textures qualities and features into the Movie.

Our documentary film for how to create a plan for "wealth in a decade" now becomes just a slicker way to trick and deceive people.[*1] Just as a producer and director's attitude permeates a Movie so do the higher frames of our mind permeate down through the things playing on the theater of our mind.

These higher frames (meta-states) make up our *attitude,* our neuro-semantic reality, and the matrices of our mind. They have no immediate connection with anything "out there." They are our mental framing of information as we build up the higher levels of our mind. In this way we put a twist on every Movie that we play.

The idea of layering frames upon frames on our Movies describes a unifying structure that suggests meaningful ways to explain, understand, and work with the higher layers of our minds. It unifies how to think about how to gain transformational leverage over the neuro-semantic system for greater personal resourcefulness.

What do you *believe* about health and fitness? Suppose you believe "Physical fitness is just a fad, it really doesn't work. Body weight is determined solely by genetics." Believe *that* and guess what attitude will come out in any fitness program you learn to represent?

Movie Making Levels
Now you know about the levels of mind. First, we use the sensory or empirical language to track information from words, whether precise or vague, into our mind-body systems to create our Movies and to supply them with a language sound track. When language is vague and non-sensory we use the indexing questions to make them more specific. As we track from words to internal Movie, we also pick up information from non-verbal features like

physiology, actions, tones, gestures, use of space, volume, etc. we also use them in the filming of our internal films.

At a higher level the words also suggest the thinking patterns that direct the Movies and edit the films. This enables us to identify the frames for our Movies, the information that governs the editorial, director, and producer levels. We use this information for how to cinematically edit the Movie.

The words imply the higher states or frames of mind which make up our attitudes, the very attitudes that we use to produce the Movies. They establish the frame of mind we use for our purpose, intention, motivation, design, quality, etc. Via meta-states we input information about the value frames, belief frames, identification frames, decision frames, history frames, expectation frames, etc.

Summary

- There are levels within a Movie and these correspond to the levels in our mind, especially in how we can think and feel about our thoughts and feelings. Technically this is called meta-cognition and is here an expression of the Meta-States model.
- It takes a hierarchy to make a Movie—actors, camera people, editors, directors, and executive producers. In our mind, because we play all of these roles, the more flexibility we have in moving up and down these levels, the more control and choice we have in running our own brain.
- It's not enough to video-record some event, we have to keep playing it. At the director level of our mind, we have to support it. What you are currently playing in the theater of your mind has higher layers of thought and emotion that

support it. Frequently we have to change that before we can change the Movie.

Endnotes:

[*1] In our training on wealth building, *Games Wealthy People Play,* we not only present a plan for how to become financially independent in a decade, but also the supporting higher frames of mind that allow it to fit our higher values and goals.

Chapter 8

PERFORMING MOVIE MAGIC

Transforming Horror Movies

For Joyful Learning

Consider someone with a phobia. Just *how* does a person create or install a phobia? How can a person *just by thinking* about some trigger (i.e., a snake, elevator, flying, speaking in public, confronting a boss, etc.) experience their whole body in a state of utter terror? How can a person freak out with so much fright? How is it possible to signal the body to experience such emotions? How does all of this work?

It's simple. All we have to do is entertain a really good *Horror Movie* in full sensorama of appropriate sights, sounds, and sensations in the Cinema of the mind. That will do it. See something horrible. Hear something terrifying. Bring it closer. Make it bigger. Step into it and be there. If you do that you will fill your body with fright. Without an exception, we have found this true for every single person suffering from a phobia that we have worked with in the past twenty years. People who are phobic have a marvelous strategy for scaring the hell out of themselves. In fact, they typically go around the world ready to jump any picture that someone suggests of pain, threat, or danger.

Suppose you wanted to model that. You would only need to ask lots of questions about the mental Movie.

> What are you seeing? How big is this picture? How close? Is it in color or black-and-white? Is it a snapshot, two-dimensional, and flat or is it a three-dimensional Movie? Any sound track? What music or words? What is the tone, volume, tempo, and pitch of this sound track? Any smells or tastes? Are you inside the Movie and experiencing it or are you sitting outside of it and watching it like a spectator?

Questions like these enable us to understand *what* the person is internally representing and *how*. By recognizing the cinematic structure of the experience, we also facilitate the person to recognize the frames and the frameworks that govern the emotions of fear. Emotions are not mysterious. They do not just come out of the blue. They make perfect sense *given* the Movie. The questions also invite the person to learn how to become their own internal movie director.

The *movie magic* we perform with NLP and Neuro-Semantics is that of taking charge of the Movie from the editor, director, or producer's position. Stepping up to that place enables us to begin to truly choose about how to encode our audio-video tracks.

> How about pushing that picture back so that you have ten rows between you and the Movie?
> What if you made it a black-and-white snapshot?

It's not that we refuse to look at the Movie. It's that we learn to look at it *while staying resourceful and empowered.* That's the key. Like the television programs and documentaries that reveal how the directors create "the movie magic" in the visual effects, we also can learn how to create internal visual effects, auditory effects, and other sensory effects that make our internal world more magical.

That's important. When we have a dramatic and exciting internal world, it affects and governs our external world of behaviors, emotions, speech, relationships, and the things that we externalize. Actually, our external world can be no more bright, positive, healthy, fun, loving, successful, etc. than the Movie playing in the cinema of our mind.

Slaying a Dragon Movie
Terri, now that we know about the *"You Shouldn't Be" Movie* that you recorded and play on the screen of your mind, how many more times do you need to play that video before you've had enough?
> I've had enough! I don't need it anymore.

No, no... I don't think you've had it enough. I think you need to feel more pain, more hurt, more hopelessness, and more desperateness!
> No, I have. I really have!

No you haven't. You can't make a vivid Movie of yourself as the star in the Movie of *Unconditional Worthiness* ... and step in there and feel, fully feel, that your value and dignity is a given and look at your mother and say, "I'm sorry that you had an old script about boys and girls ... but that has nothing to do with me."
> (Tearing up) ... That's hard.

Do you want it? Do you believe it?
> Yes, I do.

Then step into that Movie ... into the Star who knows that her value as a human being cannot be taken away by anything, especially the limitations of others ... step in there. Now turn on the new screen play and hear the strongest and most confident voice say, "I am a Somebody. I don't have to become a Somebody, I was born a Somebody with value, and dignity, and worth."
> I want to say that, I really do.

What stops you from saying it?
> I'm afraid that I won't know how to be myself. I don't know how to live with unconditional self-esteem.

That's right. And why should you? You haven't been rehearsing that script. But now you are beginning to rehearse a new script. And that's the key. Do you want to?
> Yes.

That doesn't sound very convincing.
> Yes!

See, that sounds wimpy. Say it with some power.
> *Yes I do!*

Are you ready to say "No!" to the old script, the old voice, the old Movie?
> Yes I am.

Then say "No!" to it. Refuse it. Do you know how to be stubborn? To stubbornly refuse to put up with that crap any more? (Yes) Then use that stubbornness for something useful. Stubbornly say "No!" to that old Movie.

No.   No!   NO!

There you go. And how many more times do you need to say "No!" until it registers, really registers inside? Say it. And keep doing so until that old Movie is *no longer welcomed*. Refuse it. ... Now say "Yes" to practicing and rehearsing the new one. And is your "Yes" welcoming it in so that it feels good ... feels right?

Yes.

Using Your Mind's Movie Magic

There are many patterns and processes that allow us to perform Movie Magic in our mind-and-body system. The one included here is for curing and neutralizing phobias and panic attacks. It was developed more than twenty-five years ago by the developers of NLP.   In the years since then tens-of-thousands, perhaps hundreds of thousands, of people have experienced the surprising effect of a phobia suddenly disappearing.

Yet this pattern is good not only for fears and phobias, you can use it to work wonders to get near-instantaneous relief from frightening images that recruit you, for negative films, and for any cinema that induces unpleasant emotions. It's really pretty amazing.

Visiting Your Personalized Horror Movie Show

Since we normally are *inside* our Movies and play the role of the chief actor, we can re-design our Movies so that we can *step out* of them and experience the Movie in other ways, as an observer, editor, or producer on the set. When we create our Movies and *step into them*, we associate into the thoughts, body sensations, and perceptions *as if we are there,* as if we are fully and completely there. And since our body just goes along for the ride, depending on the Movie playing in our theater, what a ride that can be!

When we watch a Movie from the first row seat of being the star actor, we play the *Be There Now Game*. As we step into the actor's role of any given memory it signals all of our brain-body parts to fully re-experience all of the thoughts and emotions that go along with the memory.

The game plan for this is simple. Step into the *Fearful Movie of Personal Horror and Dislike* and fill up your body with fear, utter terror, dread, and heart pounding anxiety. You get to go to the Movies and don't have to pay an entrance fee. But you will have to pay an exit fee. You will pay it in terms of loss of health and vitality in your mind, emotions, and body.

Stepping Out of the Movie

Whenever we play the *stepping into game* we simultaneously and inevitably play the *stepping out game*. They go hand in hand. We step into painful memories, we step out of calm resourcefulness. We step into joy and laughter, we step out of depression and being a sourpuss. It's a two-step game: step in and step out. Content is not included, you have to supply that.

When we step out from a painful memory, we frequently turn on a Movie that psychiatrists call "Dissociation." They think it's a bad Movie. They even list it as a "personality disorder" in their bible that records all of the ways to get messed up mentally (the DSM-IV). They assume that when you step out, you have to *forever stay out of all emotions.* Foolish doctors.

Dissociating, or stepping out, from an ugly memory enables us to not signal and therefore not process all of the body sensations with the corresponding emotions of the memory. We can see and hear the information while maintaining a calm, mindful, resourceful perspective. And that, in a nutshell, is the structure of the way to resolve or cure a phobia. To do this we operate from the radical idea of accessing our best resources when we deal with the information that involves thinking about horrible things without confusing those thoughts with the reality of being there. We can *just think* about them. And we can do such thinking from a state of resourcefulness—   with courage, confidence, esteem, calmness, etc.

When we run the Movie of *Just Watching an Old Horror Movie from a Place of Resourcefulness,* we utilize the power of dissociation (from the threat and danger states) and the power of association (into calmness, recognition of reality, distinguishing past/ present, etc.). Playing this *Phobia Re-Editing Movie* permits us to erase the negative emotional impact of memories that we no longer need. This frees our mental and emotional energy so that it doesn't have to keep working over "unfinished business." We finish with it, shake our hands of it, and get on with life.

Once you have produced the basic screenplay for this Movie, you can then play it all by yourself whenever you need it. But before you become that masterful with the pattern, typically you will need someone to play the director so that you just experience how the Movie goes.

How to Produce and Direct the—
Neutralizing Old Movies Movie

Step 1: Get resourceful before you start filming.
Are you ready to produce this Movie? Readiness to do so entails caring about doing this and wanting to neutralize those old Movies so that you can move on in life. If so, then you'll need your playfulness and curiosity. You'll also need a nice calm and relaxed state where you are clear-headed. You'll need that for

some of the editing and directing that you'll do that will solve old problems and perspectives. The more motivated and centered you are, the better.

> When are you at your best?
> Imagine being there fully and completely right now.
> What is that like? Just notice on the inside... How do you know you are in a motivated, centered, focused, mindful state?
> What is your breathing like, posture, facial expression, tone of voice...

When you've accessed your most resourceful states, then put your whole body into a stance that reflects such. Stand, walk, and sit as if fully in that state. Breathe, look, speak, move, gesture with all of that resourcefulness surging within you. As you ampify this state, use a physical touch or gesture or movement that you can use as your special trigger for this state. That will give you a way to anchor it whenever you need it.

Another part of the game plan for producing, directing, editing, and acting in your new Movies is the ability to *step out* of the Movie whenever you need to. We call that a state or pattern interrupt. It's like all other kinds of interrupts that jar us from a state of mind and emotion. It temporarily shifts us to another focus and so keeps us in control of our choices. So what interrupts you? What can you set up as a trigger for interruption? A coaches' whistle, a call for "Time-Out!"? Standing on your head?

Step 2: Set some awesome frames before you start.
The ability to film a fearful event and to keep it alive in your mind-body system for years, even decades, is actually a pretty amazing achievement, especially when you think about all the

things we forget. Recording a film of fear and terror and being able to step into it so that Steven King is envious is a form of accelerated learning.

Consider also the ability to have the hell scared out of you and to then link it to a tone, voice, word, object, event, etc. so that you *never forget* to freak out when you think about that trigger! That's amazing, don't you think?

Now that you know that your Movies affect your emotions, behaviors, response patterns, when we change the Movie, it's going to have extensive and pervasive transforming influences throughout your whole mind-body system. Mostly this process will neutralize that old Movie so that you'll just eliminate it from your archives of old videos. Is that okay with you?

- Who will you be without this *Fear Movie* and response?
- How will this transform your everyday life?
- How will it make a difference tomorrow?'"

Step 3: Pull out the Terror Video and step out.

What's the fear? What is the phobia about? As you pull out the fear video in your mind, put it upon the screen in your mind and step out as if you were in a movie theater. As you imagine yourself in a movie theater, put the first scene of the Movie as a still snapshot up on the screen and get yourself comfortable in a seat in the tenth row. In your mind float to that position and settle down comfortably where you can sit back and watch it. Smell your bag of popcorn or some other special treat and enjoy getting ready to see it for the last time.

Now with that snapshot on this screen, if there's any color in it, let that fade out until it is just a black-and- white photograph of that younger you. Do you see that younger you? Do you see what that person was wearing? The place where it happened?

Step 4: Step out a second time by floating into the projection booth.

Having already *stepped out* of the old Movie once to observer position, we now want to do that one more level so that we can float back and up into the projection booth were we can make editorial changes.

Experience the sensation of the feelings of *floating out of your body* there in the tenth row as you *float back and up* to the projection booth. ... That's right. Float all the way back... until you can see the back of your present day self watching the snapshot on the screen.

And enjoy the feeling of putting your hands on the plexiglass separating you from the self observing you in the tenth row watching the snapshot of the younger you on the screen with the full knowledge that a cinematic transformation is shortly to take placc.

From the editor's position you can use your hands at any time to gesture at these other locations. You can pantomime the feeling of being behind a protective plexiglass, safe and secure, and able to take full control of the Movie and all of its editorial features. And you can feel really safe here because this is the editing room. Here you can edit your films to make them more sane and healthy.

Step 5: Review the fearful cinema for the last time as you watch it to the end.

Just let the snapshot on the screen become a black-and-white Movie and review the old terror or fear or trauma to the end of the show ... Just let it play out and you can let it run as you watch it from here in the projection booth through whatever hurtful, ugly, unpleasant, even traumatic events ... just observing, just watching, and just feeling safe and comfortable *outside* the Movie ... because you are no longer in it, but just observing it and so let the scenes play out ... all the way to the end ... and then let it play out a little further until you see to some scene of comfort or pleasure ... Some time after the terror when you were with friends and having some fun or relaxing or something like that ...

Now if at any time you feel a pull that invites you to step back into the Movie, just feel the plexiglass in front of you and know that you can just watch in the safety and protection of this editing room because the Movie is about a younger you in another time and place, and you are safe here today.

If at any time you need to have the Movie move more quickly through scenes, do so... you are just observing the events as an onlooker... When the trauma is over... go to a scene where you're okay, when things are fine. Perhaps you're enjoying a hot bath or shower, a vacation, a party, reading a book, something of comfort and pleasure.

Step 6: Stop. Intermission Time.
Now after you have come to the scene of comfort, freeze frame that event and stop for a moment. Good. You got through it ... for the last time. In just a moment you are going to do something really weird. An explanation will come later, but for now just listen to the instructions about what to do. When you have a clear sense of the way we're going to play with this old Terror Cinema in your head, then it will be time to do it.

In just a minute, *step into the comfort scene* or the scene of pleasure at the end of the Movie ... and just be there fully—seeing, hearing, feeling, smelling, tasting through your own eyes, ears, and skin. Stepping into the Movie and being the actor in all of that comfort and pleasure. And be sure to let everything turn into living color. Then, when you're ready, *while inside the Movie*—push the fast re-wind button and let it zoom to the beginning in super fast rewind so that it takes all of one or two seconds. Zoom. And you're *inside the comfort* when this happens ... so that everything goes backwards, including you... Zooming for the beginning black-and-white snapshot.

Ready? Go! ... and zooooommmm!
There you go. Good. Alright, interrupt your state ... blow that whistle ... stand on your head ...

Step 7: Play it Again, Sam!

Running your Movie backwards while you're an actor inside it from a place of comfort is a strange thing and it takes the brain a little bit to learn this one, so repeat this process five to eight more times. Start at the comfort or pleasure scene and run it backwards. Each time when you step in at the end and rewind all the way back to the first snapshot ... let everything — sounds, sights, feelings, sensations, everything go backwards faster and faster and faster .... It's important to interrupt your state at the end.

As you do, then open your eyes, clear your mental screen. Then, *step into the comfort scene* at the end again, and before you can think about it, do a fast rewind from inside. It's a ride! So blast through it.

How did you like that? Open your eyes. It's over. Good.
Hey, let's do that again. *Step into the Comfort scene* again... yes,

it's such a bother! But humor me. Okay, are you fully there? Ready for the Super Fast Rewind? Zooooommm.

Step 8: Test for Movie-emotion effects.
After you have run the Movie backwards from inside it five to eight times, it's time for us to test things. We specifically want to find out if you can play the old *Terror Movie* and get your body full of fright. So try it. See if you can turn on the phobia. Try really, really hard ... as hard as you can to see if you can get the phobia feelings back.

No? Not as much. Well try harder. Still no? Well, imagine the next time something in your future may trigger it as it has in the past. Try to see if that will get it back.

Stepping In and Out of Your Movies
How does this process work?
What are the ingredients that make this process neutralize old Movies that rattle us?

What happens in *stepping* out of the old Movie is that we take a different perspective, and doing this repeatedly increases our awareness. It cues us to frame things from a different set of understandings and emotions. At the same time it sets new frames —those of safety, distance, control, not-now, past, etc.

It's these new frames that influence the old Movie. Now we can actually do something that we could not do before—*face* the old information and *think about* it in a new and different way. As long as we were inside the old Movie, we could only do one thing, be the actor and play out the old screen play.

Now we can do many new things. One of the most amazing is

that we can just observe the old information. *Just observe.* That's a description for what it means to become more objective and to not take things personal. It's hard to not take things personally when you are the actor inside the Movie. Yet it is easy to not take it personally when you are on the outside watching, eating popcorn, or in the projection booth.

In changing the frames, in expanding the frames, in adding many new resourceful frames, now the Movie is different. As a consequence, this *Re-Winding Old Movies* process reduces the emotional impact of old traumatic events as it frees us for a new way to respond.

Changing your Neuro-Theater
How does this work in the body and nervous system so that we actually feel different?

We have already noted that neurologically, *the way* we encode information governs what our brain and mind levels do with the information. If we *encode* a memory or an imagination as a cinema that fits all of the semantic frameworks so that we get the message from the director that this is "Real, Now, Immediate, Threatening, Dangerous, About Me," etc., that's what we experience.

So the way we encode how we represent things makes all the difference in the world in terms of how we respond in our emotions, skills, abilities, perceptions, etc. It means that we create our worlds of meaning. When we step into Movies, it means "real, now, immediate, etc." When we step out, it means we are editing, directing, observing, producing, play acting, or whatever role we have stepped into. We create our meanings by how we encode and frame things. So, when we change the code, we change the experience. It is as simple as that, it is as complicated as that.

Stepping in and out of the Cinemas in our minds governs what we experience. If we have had enough of old fearful, terrifying, or traumatic Movies, we can step out of them and re-wind them. We can set frames over the old Movie that says, "Not Now, No Longer Real, Past and Not Present, Non-Threatening, Not-Dangerous, Not about the Real Me," etc.

This process sets up many frames that stop the old Movies from recruiting us to play it again. What are these frames? Among them are the following:

- Just Observing and not Participating
- Watching with Dispassionate Interest
- Watching at a Distance
- Watching from my more Resourceful Self in Today
- Watching as if an Editor of the Old Movies
- Taking control of my watching ... watching it as a black and white snapshot, and an old Movie, as a Movie I can forward to a Scene of Comfort and Pleasure
- Taking control of the old Movie by Rewinding it from the Inside
- Rewinding it and washing Comfort and Pleasure backwards into it
- Taking control by teaching my brain to go from Fear and Trauma to Comfort and Rewind

With all of those messages setting the frame for *how to think and feel* about things, is it any wonder that it completely reformulates the old fear?

Other Ways to Edit the Old Terror Movie

Now that you know the basic set-up for this pattern that blows phobias to smithereens, there's certainly other fancy editorial moves that you can add to spice up the fun. The principle here is this:

> If you're not having fun "running your own brain" you haven't caught on to true mastery yet.

After *Step Four* when you have floated into the projection booth, and before you play the old Movie to the end and rewind it from inside, you can play around with editing the Movie doing any of the following.

Step into a resourceful memory.

Recall a time when you felt really creative, confident, courageous, powerful, etc. See what you saw at that time and step into it so fully that the brightness increases and you begin to glow there in the projection booth. When you are into this fully, step onto the screen with all of this and then as a most resourceful actor step into the scene where the negative trigger or fearful experience is. As you step back into the Movie resourcefully, notice how the resourceful state changes the Movie ... the actions ... the responses. It's like a super-hero arriving on the scene. Watch as this new influence transforms the old Movie giving that younger you all the resources you needed to handled that situation.

Juice up your sound track.

From the projection booth, step behind the machinery and computers and re-process your voice and all of the other sounds that make up the sound track of the old Movie. Juice it up so that your voice becomes strong, powerful, firm, courageous... give it the qualities that will make the difference. Add a laugh track, circus music, Donald Ducks' voice to the scary persons. Do whatever you need to do so that the way others sound become funny, silly, ridiculous, weak, and the way you sound becomes the dominating sounds.

Access and apply a spiritual faith.
Perhaps the resource you need is a belief in God, in angels, in an intelligent universe, whatever.   So, if you believe in a loving heavenly Father, then split your screen and see through the eye of your faith your Guardian Angel hovering over the earthly scene of your memory.   See and hear your Angel caring and loving you. Perhaps you hear, "I am with you." "I will help you." See Jesus touch you with his healing hand.

Recode the old Movie symbolically.
For instance, you might want to make the people in your memory transparent. Or color them according to how you think-and-feel about them: black, white, golden, blue, green, etc.. Draw a line around the people to make them more cartoon-like, make one your Charlie Brown, Lucy, or Snoopy, etc.

Add silly and humorous things to the Movie.
Since laughter improves the quality of life, games, mind, etc., and gives us a sense of distance from hurt, use your humor so that you can laugh.   Often we say that one day we'll look back on this and laugh. Why wait? Why not do that now? Play that Game. Zoom out into your future far enough so that you can look back and laugh.

The Magic of Transforming Our Movies
There's an artistry in learning how to use the skills and patterns for directly changing our mental Movies.   When we learn the patterns, adopt the attitudes, and then develop the confidence, then the artistry emerges.   Doing so then gives us a way to take charge

of the commands we send to our body.

The first step in all of this is *awareness*. We can't edit the Movie until we recognize them and develop awareness of them.
>*What* are we seeing, hearing, and representing?
>What Movie is playing?

After awareness comes practicing *Movie editing skills* and altering the Movie's higher frames. This involves learning the range of cinematic features and then giving ourselves to playing and experimenting until we get the hang of it.
>What are the key *features* of the visual, sound, or sensation tracks?
>What fine tuning could I do that would transform things?
>What *frames* are you using as you think *about* that Movie?

Then, above and beyond all that comes the spirit or attitude of curiosity, playfulness, exploration, recognition that it's just our mental mapping, etc.

Summary

- We can perform Movie Magic in our minds. Magic lies at our command if only we really notice the form and structure of that magic and learn some of its secrets. Then transforming frogs into princes becomes the kind of magic we can do before breakfast.
- This is the beginning of how to perform Movie Magic, but it is only that, the beginning. There's much more to come.

Chapter 9

EDITORIAL PREROGATIVES

Being the Editor-in-Chief Of your Cinema Mind

"Eat Your Heart Out, Stephen Spielberg!"

Having noticed and explored several levels in our cinema productions, from actor, to camera position, to editor, director, producer and executive, we have been learning the ins and outs of our Cinema Mind. Each level provides a different perspective, focus, and emotion. Each position carries with it strengths and weaknesses. Each level empowers us with additional ways to take charge of our MovieMind.

The last chapter explored the art of performing movie magic on horror and trauma Movies. We noticed the power of transformation that lies at the level of editing our Movies. There we used several editorial options that can have simply magical effects upon our minds and emotions. Now it is time to *rise up* to assume even fuller editorial prerogatives.

The cinematic features of our Movies are *the qualities* that give our sensory representations their qualities and properties. It is at this level that we zoom in and out with our camera perspectives. We can dim the lights or turn them on full blast. We can turn the voices down, the screeching tire sounds up, we can add in narrator's voices, flash words across the screen ... the options are abundant. We noted many of the abundant options in chapter five when we first edited an old *Insult Film*.

Yet what these cinematic features *mean* are not governed by what they are. What does dimming the lights mean? Well, it depends if we're playing a fearful Movie scene in a dark basement searching for a murderer or a romantic candlelight dinner scene. Contexts larger than the immediate effects govern the meanings of the cinematic features.

It's for this reason that we say that the cinematic effects that we paint and edit into our Movies actually are governed by a higher or meta-level. The higher frames set *the semantic significance.*

Cinematic Effects Set Meaning Frames

The distinctions that we identify as the editorial features to our Movies such as close/far, bright/dim, color or not, loud/quiet, etc. structurally format our mental Movies. These are the very features that we can edit to give our Movies the structure, the format, and the effects that we want.

In the phobia re-editing pattern of the last chapter, we floated up to the projection booth where we could edit the trauma or terror Movie so that we could just watch it without experiencing emotional reactions. How did we gain the semantic sense of "distance" and safety?" These words refer to conceptual realities. So what are the empirical features of the Movie that "stood for" (symbolically) these ideas? We used snapshot, black-and-white, up on the screen, out in the tenth row of the theater, being an audience member, etc.   These cinematic features *semantically* communicated and signified that we had "psychological distance" from the content of the Movie.

Is "distance" or "fuzziness" *inside* the Movie?
       No.
These are the conceptual *frames* that we apply to, or edit into, the Movie. They are the structural coding, or re-coding, that allows the Movie to *mean* something different to us and so trigger a different set of responses.

What about the *concept* of feeling comfort or pleasure and rewinding a Movie in fast speed? Is that the content of the Movie or our framing?   Run your brain that way and your neuro-semantics change. That's the magic.

These features (distance, fast rewind, fuzziness, etc.) are distinctions we bring to our thoughts that give us a way to *symbolically* alter the contextual frames within which the content of the Movies play out. The cinematic features are the frames that we put on the Movie, first level meta-frames. We use them to recode or re-edit our Movies.

In this way, we have a way to *symbolically* or *semantically* encode higher concepts.   It's in this way that we operate at the level of director or producer and bring our frames, attitudes, and intentions down and install them in the Movie.   In actual movies, we recognize great directors and producers precisely for their ability to do this. They have the ability to catch a vision of the effects they want to create and translate so that what we see and hear and feel on the screen puts that vision in us.

We too have higher level ideas, concepts, visions, purposes, intentions that we would like to translate from the conceptual and abstract level and install in our Movies. To do that, we use our editorial skills and prerogatives. Then we can translate the non-things of our nominalizations into see, hear, feel, smell, or taste representations on the screen.

Recognizing this starts us on the journey of becoming skillful and confident as we work with and handle these distinctions. Eventually we become more skilled in framing our cinemas and using the cinematic features for different effects. It all begins with using what we now know about how we structure our experiences using these features.

The structural change that we use in such magical patterns like the Re-Winding Pattern involve using various cinematic features for encoding and re-coding the frames that we have been using.

Cinematography of the Mind — 101
We cannot access and use our editorial prerogatives unless we know what rights and opportunities we have. What can we do? What are the choices before us? How can we influence our mental Movies?

The Visual Track of Images, Snapshots and Movies:

Brightness:	Dull	—	Bright
Focus:	Fuzzy	—	Clear
Degree of Color:	Light/ Pastel	—	Bright/ Bold
Particular Color:	Disliked	Liked	Favorite
Fact of Color:	Black-and-White	Full Color Range	
Size:	Small	Life size	Large
Distance:	Far	—	Close
Contrast:			
Movement:	Still	—	Full of Action
Direction/Location:	Right	Center	Left

	Above	—	Below
	Tilted	—	Straight on
	Up	Middle	Down
Salience of Figure:	Foreground	—	Background
Frames:	Snapshot —	Movie	
	Still Picture	—	Moving Film
Number of Images:	Single	—	Multiple
Edges of Pictures:	Bordered —	Panoramic	
Shape/ Form:	Normal, Fisheye, Flattened, etc.		
Horizontal & Vertical Perspectives:	Ratio		
Perspective:	Associated	—	Dissociated
	Actor Position	Multiple Camera, Editor, Director, Producer, etc.	
Dimensionality:	Flat 2-D image	—	3-D, holographic

The Auditory Track of Sounds, Noise, Music and Words:

Content:	What is said		
Pitch:	Low	—	High
Location of Sounds:	Front/ Back; Up/ Down; Panoramic, Single Source		
Nature of Sounds:	Continuous	—	Interrupted, On-and-Off
Tone Quality:	Pleasant	—	Unpleasant
	Cacophony		Harmony
Tone Style:	Accent		
Inflection:	What inflection used?		
Number of Sources:	One	—	Many
Perspective:	Associated	—	Dissociated
Tempo:			
Volume:	Low	—	High
Rhythm:	Noise (no rhythm) —		Presence of Rhythm
Duration:	On-and-off	—	Endures
Distance:	Close	—	Far
Clarity:	Vague, Fuzzy	—	Crystal Clear
	Unintelligible	—	Intelligibility
Whose Voice:	Identification of Voice: Self, Real, Imagined, Invented		
Music: What Music?			
Melody:			

The Linguistic Track of Words and Sentences:

Location of Words:	Above/ Below; Single source/ Multiple		
	As Sound Track	—	As Visual Images
Level:	Sensory Based	—	Evaluative
	Simple, Empirical	—	Complex
Source:	From Self	—	From Others

The Kinesthetic Track of Sensations and Feelings:

What sensations:	Warmth, Movement, Pressure, etc.		
Pressure:	Light	—	Intense, Heavy
Location:	Where on Body or in Body?		
Extent of sensation:	Local	—	Pervasive
Moisture:	A Little	—	A Lot
Shape:	Scattered, pin-point, round, up-and-down, etc.		
Texture:	Rough	—	Smooth
Temperature:	Cold	Warm	Hot
Movement: Kind and Nature —			
Duration:	Momentary	Repeating	Continuous
Intensity:	Light	—	High
Frequency:	Time / Pattern	—	
Rhythm:	—	—	
Smells:	—	—	
Tastes:	Sour / Sweet	Bitter / Salty	

Cinematography Factors

Transitions: Fading in / Fading out,

Time Transitions indicating time passing, seasons occurring, time lapses

Flashback dramatization

Spotlight moving and holding on central figure: close-up shots, blurring out other figures with spotlight of clarity on the central figure. Backlighting

Juxtaposing time sequences: Present/ Past / Future

Collage	Juxtaposition of unrelated images
Montage	Juxtaposition of related images, images that have been put together as a selective choreography of separate images orchestrated for a purpose.
Mood Framing	Framing to create special moods.
Pixillation	A computerized process that omits two out of three frames of action to create a surreal jumpy look. The effect is similar to that associated with a flashing strobe light at a discotheque.
Superimposition	Superimposing one imagine upon another.

Multiple Screens: split screen with two screens, six screens, etc.

Hand-held camera shot that follows the action, moving through house, or on roller-coaster, etc. to give the sensation "You are there!"

De-Commissioning Your "Mind Police"

"But is it right to change your memories?"

"Aren't we supposed to keep our memories accurate to what happened? If we don't, how can we tell what's real?"

These are but a few of the fears that many people have prevents them from assuming their editorial prerogative. How about you? Do you have permission to re-edit your thoughts, memories, or understandings? Or has someone *forbidden* and tabooed you from doing so? Are you afraid that "The Mind Police" will come and get you if you change your memories?

Have no fear. It's *your* brain and you can do with it anything you want. No Mind Police will come after you. They will not pound on your doors late at night, ready to arrest and interrogate you for fooling around with the images in your mind. *What* you remember and *how* you have encoded that memory is your business.

This raises the *quality control* questions that we'll explore more fully in the next chapter. Ultimately, do you have a video-record of past events that *support* your resourcefulness or that *undermines* or even disables it? Do you hold memories as referent experiences that make you more alive and vital, more creative and loving, more productive and successful— or do you keep on file Movies of terror, dread, anxiety, fear, self-contempt, trauma, etc.? If so, *why* in the world are you doing that?

Don't default to the lame excuse, "Because it happened." Give me a break. Sure it happened, and sure you filmed it, but *why* are you keeping it? Why are you *using those videos* as references for today and the future? After all, it's your brain and you are the one doing it in this moment and this day.

Does it enhance your life? Does it make things in your internal world more pleasant, positive, and empowering?
"But what if it happens again?"

That's like saying you really hate cut-and-slash horror Movies and least you happen to watch them again, you better keep the videos really close to you. The problem with this is that the old Movies become zip-files and wallop you really good in a nanosecond.

Yet, if it is a trashy video of hurtful, traumatic, hateful, and ugly events—*why* keep it around? Do you really need it?

"But what will I play on the theater of my mind if I don't have *that*?"
Ah, there's the question.

Editorial Movie Magic
Co-founder of NLP, Richard Bandler conversationally offered the following comments about a phobia. Read this piece to get an understanding of it; then re-read it to see if you can recognize the structure of what he's doing in terms of the Movie you have to make in your mind to understand it.

> "It's an amazing thing to be able to remember to get terrified every time you see a spider. You never find a phobic looking at a spider and saying, 'Oh damn, I forgot to be afraid.' Are there a few things you'd like to learn that thoroughly? When you think about it that way, having a phobia is a tremendous learning achievement." (1985, p. 11)

So, did you notice what went on cinematically in your mind as you read that statement?
If not, then read it again and notice how you make sense of it. It starts with a statement that's shocking to our normal way of thinking and so it has a tint of humor in it.

> "It's an amazing thing to be able to remember to get terrified every time you see a spider."

Representationally, the first line invites us to "see a spider." That's the Movie. And referentially, his comment frames "seeing a spider" as a member of the class of something to "get terrified" about. Yet, just prior to introducing that category, he introduced yet a higher frame, "Remember to get terrified." In those four words there are *frames by implication.* For instance, they suggest that "getting terrified" is a task, something that you have to do, something to remember, something that not everyone can do. And all of those "frames by implication" have a tempering and texturing effect on the film that we're creating in our mind, do they not?

Yet there's more. Just prior to that is the line, "It's an amazing thing to be able to ..." So before the Movie starts we are *preframed* with three levels:
1) Amazing feat
2) Able to remember
3) To get terrified every time.

Then comes the Movie. "Seeing a spider."
To then give vividness, humor, and compellingness to the Movie, Bandler says, "You never find a phobic looking at a spider and saying, 'Oh damn, I forgot to be afraid.'" How about that for giving some specific details to the Cinema playing in our seeking-to-understand mind? And the ridiculousness of that mini-scene makes the imagery all that much more memorable.

Finally, to *post-frame* the idea, he adds a couple more lines that set an even higher frame *about* the whole Movie.
> "Are there a few things you'd like to learn that thoroughly? When you think about it that way, having a phobia is a tremendous learning achievement."

Above the previous frames we now have:
>   4) Such thorough learning and a tremendous learning achievement.

Isn't it amazing that so much can be said in so few words? This is the wonder and magic of language and especially of casting a spell. I mean producing a Movie in our minds that can create a problem or innoculate us from toxic thinking-and-feeling.

"Hey! I'm the Editor!"

Pull out your Movie about health and fitness. Do you have one? Do you have a Movie of eating and exercising in just the right way that supports your long-term goals of health, fitness, and everyday vitality? If not, then begin to create that film. Use people who seem to know how to do that as your models. It's not rocket science. Just record what eating right, exercising regularly, taking appropriate actions for looking good and feeling great would be like.[1]

Now step back from that documentary. Is it very exciting? Is it compelling and motivating? Probably not. So juice it up. Using all of your editorial prerogatives, put in "Rocky" music, or whatever cranks your case, and make it a classic. From time to time step into the Movie to see what it does for you. Does it energize you? Does it conjure up the best states in you?

You can do the same with your Movie about self-esteeming. Do you have a great Movie about how to accept, appreciate, and esteem yourself as a valuable and worthwhile person? Unconditionally valuable? Then make your film. Then make it sensorama land so that you can step into the most challenging circumstances and they can't take your dignity away. Your dignity is a given no matter what. Make a Movie of being uninsultable.[2]

Summary

- *Your* editorial prerogative is *your* right to encode *your* Movies any way *you* want to. After all, it's *your* brain and *your* Cinema Mind. There are no Mind Police who will come and arrest you for re-editing your films.
- How you encode your Movies creates your internal semantic world —your universe of meaning that governs the games you play.

Endnotes:

[1] See, *Games Slim People Play.*

[2] These are some of the Movies that we invite people to make in our trainings in Meta-States known as *Accessing Personal Genius.* You can find this in *Secrets of Personal Mastery.*

Chapter 10

A DIRECTOR'S FRAME
OF MIND

Thinking *about* the way we use our sensory Cinema to represent what we see, hear, feel, smell, and taste in the empirical world, moves us to a higher level. Above and beyond our mental Movies are those higher levels of mind by which we create, produce, direct, and edit our films. We develop mastery over the theater of our mind by meta-thinking. When we make a meta-move we can think *about* our Movies—their qualities, features, and properties. We can establish the moods and attitudes that permeate our cinemas. We can operate as editor, director, and producer of our MovieMind.

To create a Movie, someone has to direct it. Someone has to take charge of the actions, the editing, the point of view, the camera perspectives, etc. We need a *director*. And there's a part of your mind from which you too can direct your mental Movies, is there not?

Directing the Meanings of Your Cinema

We already noted that we not only *represent* things in our mind, we also *frame* our mental Movies with meaning. We can explore the horror Movies of those people with phobias and not only find out about their *representations*, but also their meanings and *references*.

Okay, I have an idea of the terrible images and the horrible scenes that you are referring to, but what does that mean to you? What frame of reference are you using to view this? What do you think *about* that? What do you *feel* about that?

Beyond the actions and feelings in the actor level of experience, when we give things meaning we create our inner attitude or spirit. After all, some people *love* horror Movies; they buy up the latest Stephen King novel to *enjoy* being scared and frightened. Other people *play with* the terror knowing "It is just a Movie." This enables them to see the terror without it bothering them. The way they frame it governs how they respond. Is it real or unreal? Is it serious or just for fun? Is it entertainment or a real danger?

>*Our frames of mind govern the meanings* (or semantics, hence *neuro-semantics*) *that we give to things.*

What's your *frame of mind* about health, happiness, self, success, relationships, work, career, exercise, fitness, etc.? Your frame of mind determines the games that you can play. If you don't want to play the *Phobia Game,* we could first change the Movie that you play inside your head, but we could also simply go higher and change the frame of mind (the meanings) that you give to the Movie. This is where we change the beliefs, assumptions, expectations, decisions, and other frames that make up the higher levels of your mind.

Directing Your Cinematography for Resourcefulness

The cinematic productions we create in our mind gives us a new way to think about the input, processing, and output of information that we call "communication." Yet our *awareness* of such information occurs via the "languages" of the mind, our sensory representation systems appear to us as a Movie. We experience our knowledge on the screen of our mind as an internal Movie. Of course, it is not real, and yet (on another level) it is (or becomes) "real" to us since it is information in our brain-body network. That's why it affects our neurology. That's why we say it makes a difference *what* and *how* we represent things.

Directing the Quality of our Movies

What is *the quality* of your internal Movies?

Do you have some great Movies playing in the theater of your mind?

Do the quality of your Cinemas make your internal life rich, full, dramatic, fun-filled, and a delightful place to be?

Ultimately, *the quality of your life—your mind, your Movies, your states is up to you.* The good-news is that you have a tool for "running your own brain" when you run *Quality Checks* on your Movies. Quality control checks give you a way to take charge of the Movie. You can rise up in your mind as your own editor, director, producer, and executive and run a Quality Control check on the Movie.

Then, if the Movies currently playing in the theater of your mind-body system do not put you in the best states, if they do not provide you a training film for how to perform with excellence, your recognition can lead you to do something about it. Doing this puts you at choice point. Now you can choose to direct or edit new audio-video Movies.

When it comes to the quality of our lives, the problem with a low quality life comes from *the Movies* that we play. There's nothing wrong with us; it's the Cinemas that we play and respond to. If we are sick and tired of feeling scared, terrified, and timid, we have to stop playing the horror Movies in our mind and replace them with some heroic adventure films.

When we ask *quality control questions* about our Movies, we learn to think like a director.

> Does this Movie enhance my life?
> Does it bring out my best?
> Does it create the kind of thoughts and feelings that enrich my skills?
> Does this Movie create empowering motivations?

If we make sense of the world through our sensory Movies with a sound track that contains words as well as other auditory components, and the Movies we play signal our entire neuro-linguistic system about how to respond, then *why* in the world do some people watch some of the sick and disgusting Movies that they do in their heads?

> Why do they watch horror Movies?
> Why do they watch fatalistic defeatist Movies?
> Why do they create and repeatedly play videos of insult, humiliation, contempt, etc.?
> Why do others play Movies of trauma, abuse, and rage?

Why in the world are you watching *that* Movie?
These "why" questions invite us to step out of the Movie and into higher level positions so that we can explore intentions and goals. What do we really want?

The simplest answer to the "Why?" is that they are *trying* to make things better. They are *trying* to finish them, make them go away. Or they think that they have no other choice and have to keep playing them. Whatever the reason, the system is attempting to do something positive and of value for us. The problem is that it's just not working. It's just a wrong choice and understanding. This brings up a crucial principle about our neuro-semantic systems. It is an essential one to understand and use if we shall ever become masterful in managing our own minds.

> *People are always doing the best they can with the resources they have. They always have positive intentions behind even their most ugly and hurtful behavior.*

Directing the Cinemas of Your Mind

> *How* do our higher states of mind (meta-states) affect the mental Movies that play on the screen of our mind?

If our internal cinemas put us into states so that we feel fear or horror when we play fearful scenarios in our mind, joyful and playful when we play comedy routines, confident and courage and when we play heroic Movies, what happens when we have a state about a state?

> The answer is incredibly simple and yet fabulous. *These higher states set frames for our Movies.* They guide and govern the director and editor's perspectives.

Are you running an old fear film in your mind about the danger of speaking up in public, asking your boss for a raise, interviewing, etc.? That gives us clues about the Movie. But what do you think *about* that experience and your feelings about that experience? Do you *justify* your fear, *validate* it, *hate* it, *contempt* yourself for the lack of courage, *feel stuck* as if you have no other choice? These states about your states describe and install the mental and emotional *tone* of your Movie.

In terms of our mental Movie, our meta-states describe *the attitude* that we have as *the director* of our own Movies. Our meta-states texture and qualify our Movies endowing them with an affective tone. They describe our attitude (or frame of mind) as we direct our lives. So as we move up the levels, "What to you think or feel *about* that?" we identify our higher frames of mind as editor, director, producer, and executive.

If I play an *Enraged and Outraged Film* and do so with the higher frame or meta-states of shame about that, self-contempt about that, feeling out-of-control, being "made" angry by someone else, etc. then the mental Movie takes on these qualities. This introduces the dynamic complexity of how states-upon-states interface with each other. Sometimes they make the Movie stronger, *feeling justified* about my anger intensifies my anger, whereas *calm relaxation* about the anger reduces it and makes it more manageable. *Respectful of others* while angry adds yet another texture to the Movie.

Outframing Your Movie Frames
1) Identify a Movie that you've been playing in your mind that puts you in a not-so resourceful state.
    What non-enhancing state or states do you sometimes experience?
    What Movie initiates those states?
2) Take a meta-position editing stance.
    Suppose you had to continue playing this same Movie, but

could choose the attitude that you use in doing so. What attitude would you pick?

Access the state of that attitude and apply it to the state of the Movie.

3) Experience and evaluate.

As you fully experience the higher state and apply it to the Movie, how does it affect the Movie? What happens?

What other resource state or attitude would you want to use also?

4) Quality control the experience.

How well does this new attitude about the old Movie serve you?

Does it enhance your life?

Any other awareness about other resources you could bring to bear upon the old Movie?

Directing Your Life to a Higher Good

There are several reasons for *rising up in our minds* and stepping up to the perspective of director or producer of our life Movies. One of the most important is that by transcending the lower levels of information processing, we access and operate from our higher purposes, our higher intentions, our higher understandings.

Doing this allows us to get in touch with larger level perspectives, values, ideas, ideals, and visions. Doing so also allows us to avoid getting caught up in the details and seduced into dramatic Movies at lower levels. That often happens. We film the events of our lives and get caught up in the content and sometimes lose our way —saying, thinking, and doing things that do not really serve us well and that do not reflect our highest values. We may get caught up in some battle that we may not even care that much about. And even if we "win" it, the win is meaningless for the most part.

This happens to us all. We get so caught up in an argument that we begin to feel compelled to win the argument. Yet in "winning" it—what have we won? What has it really accomplished?

There's a saying about this. "Behind every behavior is a positive intention."
This means that everything we do at some higher level we do for a positive reason. It may not be positive for the person receiving the behavior, yet it is positive for the one generating it. The person is *intending*, wanting, desiring, hoping, and believing it is.

Yet while our intentions may be positive, are they really getting us the results we want? The quality control check gives us one way to think like a director and to check. Another way is to begin to run *reality checks* on our films.

The idea that every behavior is driven by a positive intention does not mean that all behavior is good and that there is no such thing as "evil," or that we should condone everything. We should not. It does *not* mean that, and that is not how we use this idea. *Positive intention* grows out of an understanding of the *systemic nature* of the mind-emotion-body-culture interaction. It also enables us to reframe meaning because we can recognize differences in the levels of our mind. That is, yes, at one level we may have meant to hurt someone, but *why* did we want to do that? Was it not that at a higher level, we felt threatened and wanted to protect ourselves? So within the same system we have a lower level intention to do harm while at a higher level an intention to protect ourselves.

Positive intention means that our behaviors, talk, actions, etc. at the primary level are driven at a higher level by a positive intention of trying to make things better. That may be a delusion.

Often it is.   It may *not* serve any positive value, in fact, it may make things a hundred times worse. The "positive intention," may only have the most superficial semblance to anything "positive."

The idea of *positive intentions* at higher levels does not validate ugly or hurtful behavior. Nor do we use it to dismiss behavior or to let someone get by with murder. Instead we *use* it to make a critical distinction, namely that we are *not* our behavior and that behavior occurs at a different level from our intentions. This helps us to avoid confusing person and behavior.

Who we *are* as persons is *not* defined *only* by what we do. We *are* much more than what we *do*. *Doing* and *being* refer to two very different experiences and different experiences at different levels.

Yes, our actions do emerge from *being*, yet our actions do not express the last word about us. How we behaved at eighteen months, three years, at fourteen, as a young adult, in middle years, etc. differs significantly. Behaviors are just expressions of a person at a given time in a given context, not our heart and soul.

We do well to remember this. If we *confuse* person and behavior we fall into the trap of "unsanity" by identifying ourselves with a behavior or experience. *Identifying* imprisons us and locks us to our actions and prevents further growing and developing.

We use *positive intention* to discover (or to create) higher and more positive value frames so that we can see ourselves and others beyond a particular behavior. Typically, we find that even the worst behaviors are performed because a person is trying to protect himself, to improve her life, to promote ideas or causes, to avoid pain, etc. The *intention* may be very well and good.

But the person's map about *how* to do that may be very faulty and lacking —impoverished. The producer or director part of our higher mind *wants* to create a beautiful and successful Movie, but the only films available are those that play out scenarios of hurt, ugliness, nastiness, evil, insult, revenge, etc. At the higher level we mean well, at the lower level we don't have an appropriate strategy or map for how to make it happen.

How is it that the hurtful or obnoxious behaviors dominate? Mostly because some lower (or primary) level film gets activated and we get so caught up in it that we can't, or don't, rise up to a higher level. This is especially true when the primary emotions of fear and anger, revenge or hurt are activated by some threat or danger. Then our first-level *attentions* are so strong and intense we cannot step out of that Movie and consult with our executive level mind to consider consequences, others, morality, ecology, health, etc. It's not that we are evil or demonic at the highest intentions, but that the more dramatic and vivid Movies are really sick and toxic, and consuming.

Frequently, at the lower levels of mind, our *intentions* may be negative, ugly, hurtful, malicious, wicked, etc. We may want to hurt another, abuse, murder, etc. But why? Why do that? What will we get when we get that? By shifting to higher levels and discovering or creating the higher *positive intentions*, we move ourselves or another beyond the negative motives. This gives a person a chance to re-map and to begin operating from a more positive intention.

Otherwise, we demonize ourselves or others, assume that "at the core" I, he, or people "are" evil, bad, demonic, etc. Assuming that we act to live, survive, be safe, enjoy, connect, love, feel good about ourselves,   contribute, self-actualize, worship, etc. (Maslow's list of human needs and drives), enables us to foster growth and to frame things so that it gives us new opportunities.

Effective communication with others (even with ourselves) and effective transformation of dysfunctional patterns begins as we assume the best and look for positive intentions. We cannot "reframe" behaviors if we don't. Reframing operates from this premise. Using this premise as editors of our Movies when we engage in therapy, business, with loved ones, parenting, etc. describes a very different attitude than what most of us have learned in our cultures. Very few of us grow up with this attitude. We usually don't even have this film in our heads. We assume that "a person *is* what he or she *does*. And that's all one is."

By way of contrast, the Movie that "a person is more than his or her behaviors" invites us to become proactive rather than reactive when something negative happens. Instead of immediately playing a "Rambo" movie of rage and revenge, we turn on a film wherein we look at things from the other's point of view first.

At the director's level of mind, we play the film, *Looking for Positive Intentions* and so step into the actor's role of taking the time and trouble to enter into the other's world, calibrate to that person's reality,   and use that as the foundation for communicating. By assuming the best, we can then use feedback as information rather than more things to react to.

Directing and Writing Your Own Screen Play
When it comes to producing and directing a great Movie, great cinematography alone is not enough. Without a good screenplay, even the best movie magic effects will not redeem it. We all

know this. We need a great story, a plot that's significant and not peripheral.

> "It's not the quality of the idea that makes a good play, it's the quality of the *dramatization* of the idea." (*The Art and Craft of Playwriting*, p. 67).
>
> "The real gold in a good idea is seldom found in the initial spark. It's found in the dramatist's *development* of the idea." (68)

So the part of our mind that chooses, writes, creates, or finds a great screenplay for our lives is that part that makes the executive decision about what to live for. It is up to the executives to choose the screenplay to turn into a Movie. Then the director, editors and actors take that script and fulfill it on the screen, so it is in our minds and lives.

The story counts. The narrative that we commission, value, and believe in will become the story that we direct and star in. This leads to many questions.

> What story or stories have you been producing?
>
> Have you quality controlled these narratives?
>
> Did you personally choose them or are they just the default stories you've grown up with and assume are normative?
>
> Do you like to be "storied" with those narratives?
>
> What story would you prefer to produce, direct, and act in?
>
> Would it be a comedy, heroic adventure, conquest, drama, melodrama, love story, or what?

The Use of Words in our Movies

We use words at two levels. Within the Movie playing in the theater of our mind there are first the words that make up *the sound track* of the things that are said in the script. Then there are the meta-frames or *the screen play* that defines what's going on. Like the words that flash across a Movie that names the Movie, or that describes the next scene.

Who establishes the screen play frame?
Is it not the writers and producers?   They are the ones to determine the script and then write the screenplay so that it fits together as a cohesive plot. This establishes the editorial style, the motivation, intention, and attitude that shows up in the actors. Language becomes increasingly important as we move up the levels. By language we stabilize and sustain the screenplay.

Frame Glue for our Movies

Creating a single shot or scenario of a Movie is one thing, but how do we create and hold together all of the frames of a Movie so that when it plays, it plays out a consistent and meaningful story? At the primary level, it's child's play to represent this and then that, and then this other. But how do we create a compelling and meaningful narrative?

We need a plot, a story, a narrative and a screen play that puts it all together.
In the mind, we use language for this.

Language is the *glue* that allows us to tie ideas together, experiences together, to create a plot, to develop a theme, to write a script that coheres over time. So again, it is the higher or meta-representation system of abstract symbols (language) that holds the frames of our scenes together. Cinematically, they function as our ongoing screen play or plot that narrates the story that we "hold in mind" and believe in.

"Behind every behavior is a positive intention."

    1) *Representationally,* how do you *represent* that?

        In the Movie of your mind, think of some behavior. See that behavior, hear it, feel it. If it is obnoxious, hurtful, and nasty behavior, then step out to watch it as an observer. Adjust the cinematic features of the Movie so that you can watch it comfortably. Now edit into the Movie the understanding that "behind" or "above" that piece of behavior, the person is attempting to accomplish some positive value of some sort for him or herself. How do you *represent* that? How do you represent layer upon layer of intentions until you find a level that's sufficiently positive?

        In the Movie in my mind, I see a person in a bubble—the bubble represents his or her state. I color that bubble so that the color symbolically represents the state (e.g., red for anger, pink for gentle, black for sad and depressed, etc.). As the Movie plays, behaviors pop out of the bubble and above and beyond the bubble I see a white aura that indicates the higher positive intentions that the person is attempting to express.

    2) *Referentially*, how do you *frame* this Movie?

        What does it mean to you? What conceptual contexts do you apply to it? When you look at your Movie of behavior having positive intentions behind it, what does this mean to you? The basic goodness of people, the possibility of creating higher intentions through using this frame, the recognition that people are more than their behaviors, etc.?

Notice how Bandler (1985) plays with the idea that "people are not broken, but work perfectly well."

        "People work perfectly. I may not like what they do, or they may not like it, but they are able to do it again and again, systematically. It's not that they're broken; they're just doing something different from what we, or they, want to have happen." (15)

Consider these lines from the standpoint of representing and referencing. On the screen of our mind, we see "people," we see people doing what people do—living, working, playing, parenting, insulting each other, being abusive and nasty, yelling, blaming, etc. This gives us *representations*. "Houston, we have a Movie." Then the word "perfectly" comes but as a qualifier for how people function, it jars things. The Movie comes to a halt, it stops. "Perfectly?" "People work perfectly?"

Then comes the line, "I may not like what they do..." Yes, that's right! This paces (or matches) my experience. Movie starts up again. People doing things ... and I not liking everything they are doing. "They may not like it..." Another pacing line. That's right. They also may dislike what they are doing. I know that one. "But they are able to do it again and again, systematically." As the Movie continues I observe the disliked behavior going on and on and on ... I not liking it, they not like it. Hey, this Movie sucks!

"Systematically... It's not that they're broken, they are just doing something different from what I (or they) want to have happen." Here's the *frame*. This is what it *means*. It works! People work perfectly. "Perfect" refers to the structured and predictable nature of the actions, that the behaviors are actually achievements, accomplishments.

Summary

- "Running our own brain" means learning how to step out of the Movies that run in our minds and step into the director's perspective. Learning to think like a director enables us to quality control our Movies to see if they really work well for us in a balanced and healthy way. It means running reality checks to see if they are pure fantasy or whether we can use them for everyday life.

- Moving to the director's position is a higher frame of mind or meta-state and involves avoiding over-identifying ourselves from the roles that we play in our Movies.

Chapter 11

COMMUNICATING CINEMA TO CINEMA

Given that we all have a Cinema or MovieMind and "make sense" of information by *representationally tracking* from words to our mental Movie, this gives us a new way to think about communication. In MovieMind talk, what is *communication?*

> Communication is evoking a Movie on another's mental screen similar to the one playing in our theater. It is transferring or copying a film from one mind to another.

When we communicate, we attempt to use words and gestures to get another person to produce a mental cinematography that accords with the one we have in mind. We use language to offer a screenplay so that the other person can see *what* we see and *how* we see it.

When we communicate well, the other says,
> "I can *see* that!"
> "I *see* what you mean."
> "I can *hear* that and it does *feel* good."

In communicating we seek to get another person to turn on a Cinema in his or her mind similar to the one in ours. The closer our mental-emotional worlds and history of referent experiences, the easier it is to do this. The more different our experiences and beliefs, the more challenging and difficult becomes the communication.

Why is that? Because we never receive the communications of others directly and simply. Rather, the "screen of consciousness" that we use to *track over* from the words of another person to our own internal Movie has default settings. We have our own way of producing, directing, and editing. We have our own *references, frames,* beliefs, values, etc. We don't even have to marshal these and consciously use them, we have learned them so well, they are now automatic. It's our reference system and style for understanding things.

That's why you can innocently tell someone a story and suddenly find that the other person has taken it all wrong and is reacting in ways that you didn't expect and didn't want.

From when we first began to see, hear, feel, etc., we even develop preferences for which senses to use (visual, auditory, kinesthetic, etc.). We develop our preference for which cinematic features to use (close/far, bright/dim, large/small, etc.). We developed our preferences for which frames to use: pains to avoid or pleasures to approach; things practical and useful or things right and correct, choices or procedures, things fun or things that bring state, etc. We even develop preferences and beliefs about why and how to produce our mental Movies: to be loved, to get approval, to be powerful, to win, to not lose, to show someone up, to be right, to just survive, to discover truth, etc.

In communicating our ideas, thoughts, and experiences to another and receiving theirs, the messages are always filtered and contaminated by our *models of the world*, that is, by our dominate cinemas and editorial styles. That's why we really never do know *how* a person is editing, directing, or producing the words and gestures we use or what Movie they record in their mind. We know how we intended the words to be used, what films we are attempting to evoke, and what cinematic features we would like the other to use. But we never know how it all gets filtered, recorded, filmed, or edited. We are not the editor or director in any other mind, at best we can only do that in our own.

Movie Contaminated Communications

This explains why we are much more likely to mis-communicate than to communicate accurately or effectively. Our mental Cinemas and cinematic settings get in the way. They get in the way as our cinema's default settings. It is in this way that our frames interfere. These are *not* just different thoughts, they actually make up our neuro-semantic reality that governs the Movies we see and can see. We actually live inside of our mind-emotion-body-culture structures that map our reality. It's not just that we *have* a "mental screen of consciousness," we mostly *live inside it* and operate from out of it. This more fully describes what we mean by "state"—our neuro-semantic states are our personal world filled up with the productions currently playing.

So what?
This "so what" is very important. We experience the world out there and the world of others *through* our Cinema as our story, our narrative, our life script, our programming, and our belief frames. All these terms and phrases describe the same phenomenon, we don't deal with the world directly, only indirectly through our maps. So as we realize this we are able to truly understand and use

this communication guideline:

> *The meaning of your communication is the response you get, regardless of your intention.*

This no-fault, non-blaming model of communication helps us open our eyes and ears, move into a state of sensory awareness so we can more clearly recognize the responses we "receive" from the other. It helps us to stop reading everything solely through our mental Movie. It helps us to recognize that there are other films playing, other stories, narratives, life-scripts, programs, beliefs, etc. This allows us to now use the "screen of our mind" in a new and powerful way. Namely, to just *track* from what others actually say and welcome their Movies inside our heads so that we can actually understand what is playing in their world.

> Did the message this person receive match the message I sent?
>
> Is the sender and the listener watching the same Movie inside?
>
> What did the receiver hear? What Movie did it evoke in that person's mind?
>
> What does the editor, director, and producer inside that person's processing style do with the screen play that I offered?
>
> What words and gestures can I use to convey the film or message I want to convey?
>
> What filters or cinematic settings influenced this person to hear and translate things in that way?

Explorative questions about the communication process enable us to *avoid* taking *mis*communication personally. They allow us to focus more exclusively on clarifying the messages and on developing the flexibility to vary our messages until we can get through. Until message sent is message received. This also highlights the importance of checking out what is happening on the inside.

What is the message received?
Does it match message sent?
How is it off?
How do I need to vary my signals?

We never "fail" in the communication process, we only and always get responses. We continually receive feedback about processing styles and the effect it has in another. If we use it as such every response becomes useful feedback.

Recognizing that everybody has their own way of filming, editing, and producing the things that occur on the screen of their mind frees us from one especially impoverishing idea. Namely, that just because we said something it has to be received in the way we said it or make sense to the other in the way we find it meaningful. Communication doesn't work that way. Knowing this frees us for greater flexibility, inquiry, and sensory awareness.

Framing the communication process in this way eliminates blame, judgment, and negative feelings. Communication is *not* moral or immoral in itself. It's just an information transfer process. There is no "right" or "wrong" way to input and process information. In communicating, we simply share symbols that stand for referents that we map onto the movie theater of our mind. And ultimately, each of us is responsible for what we do with the *symbols*. We are responsible for the meanings, frames, cinematic settings, and states that our films induce in us. We try to blame others for *making* us create our internal Movies and seeing them so that they make us feel bad, but its our brain. It's our mental Movie. It's our choice about how to represent things.

Switch to the Discovery Channel
Framing communication in this way turns the exchange of words and symbols into a *process of discovery*. It also empowers us to become more resourceful in our communicating, more professional, and over time, much more effective and persuasive.

To increase your own confidence of running, editing, directing, and producing your own internal Cinemas, use and practice this frame for a period of time. If you know that what you have been doing does not work, and you keep doing it, you will just get more of the same. Is that what you want? If not, then try something new. Something different. Anything. Experiment. By flexibly shifting our use of symbols and openly receiving and playing with the symbols of others, we increase our chance of succeeding in accurately transferring our messages and at least understanding each other.

If our Movies are forever getting in the way of cleanly sending and receiving information, and if we never know what we have communicated, then we can use the *There is no failure, there is only feedback* frame as our guideline for communicating.

This allows us to keep at it without frustration, anger, or blame. Identifying and clarifying to ourselves our message and developing a clear outcome, acting by speech and behavior, noticing results, calibrating to others, flexibly adapting to generate other responses, checking feedback, etc. And we keep at it until we succeed.

Communication — Copying a Movie
Successfully understanding others, books, trainings, and knowledge involves our skills in producing an accurate film from the information. We seek to create a copy of the film and store

it in our achieves. Of course, this depends on the degree that we can get out of ourselves and hear the other person clearly, without all our frames and settings getting in the way. When we can do that, we can film things using all of the sensory systems and with all the necessary frames that the other provides.

This doesn't mean I have to agree with the Movie, believe it, or condone it. It just means I can accurately represent it. Of course, to let it in I do have to let go of my pre-judgments and empathically seek first to understand the person or the idea. It means that I do not fear understanding another. We can playfully step into the "know-nothing" state and use the indexing questions. From there we can simply *model* the symbols offered and make a Movie of it. Later on we can evaluate it. This allows us to reproduce the content of the Movie and all of the editorial structures.

Conversationally Tracking Words to Pictures
All *successful* replication of a learning, skill, behavior, or expertise starts with pacing or *matching* the Movie that we have imported. As we accurately and vividly film a set of high quality performances and reset our frames so that we can "try it on," we can replicate the strategy to some extent.

To *successfully* learn, develop, and master anything, we employ our mental Movies to encode and represent two locations: present state and desired outcome state. From there we can then create a mental Movie of the resources that we need in order to move from one to the other.

Communicating information and meaning with another person allows us to share an experience with the other. This is not a linear process, but a non-linear one. It goes round and round. It involves feedback and feed forward loops.

We use the indexing questions as a tool to step back from the information so that we can see the layers and structure of the plot of the Movie. Then we can see the associative and contextual meanings that make up the script.

The indexing *questions* focus primarily on structure:
"How do you know that? How do you do this?"

They focus our attention on understanding the plot and narrative of the Movie. When we ask it of someone with an impoverished Movie, it exposes its weakness and invites the editor part of our mind to invent a new script.

Here we operate with a higher intention in all Movie productions. We have a Movie about seeking to understand. Our attitude is essentially *explorative.* As a tool for exploring, we use it best when we come from an attitude of empathy, when we seek to build rapport:
"Help me to understand what you're thinking and feeling, *how* do you do that or know that? What does that mean to you?"

Using the questions, we take the initiative to understand the Movies playing in the mind of another. Rather than waiting around for others to share, we proactively go first. So we enter the other's world. We model or film the other's models or internal Movies. This allows us to discover the other's patterns and style for turning our information signals into Movies.

We can do this with the most extreme examples. What Movie does a paranoid schizophrenic play in his mind? Or someone who is a multiple-personality, or a sociopath? Their sensory systems, words, language patterns, symbols, metaphors, strategies, meta-programs, meta-states, etc. give us that information. We explore their language to model and discover the frames they use about their Movies.

Sometimes it's surprising, even shocking, to discover the Movies that some people play over and over in their minds. It always makes sense. And when we know the editorial and director's patterns for how a person "makes sense" of things (their cinematic default settings), we can use those very patterns to more effectively get through to that person. We call this *pacing*. We match the other's model of the world. We use their Cinema Mind to offer a Movie they can see, hear, and feel. This makes our language especially powerful and effective. It enables us to understand, create rapport, build empathy, reduce mis-understandings, reduce conflicts, etc. Lots of good things!

Summary

- *Communication* takes on a new twist when we think about it as being a screen writer and editor to another's internal Cinema. Then we use our words to enable the other person to produce and edit an internal Cinema similar to ours. Then we use questions and feedback to keep checking on what the other is producing.
- These same factors influence learning, comprehending, and modeling.

Chapter 12

FILMING NEW SKILLS

The Art of Producing and Editing
New Resourceful Movies for our Video-Library

What goes on in our mind-and-body system when we learn a new skill?
How does learning and developing a new expertise relate to the Movies in our mind?

At the most fundamental level, every skill involves "information." To pull off any skill you have to know something about the skill. This means *representation* which then evokes *states* that are inside of *frames*. In this way, our MovieMind gives us our way to think about and sequence what we know about a particular set of behaviors. So if we want to become masterful with a skill set, we have to film *what* we will do, *how* we will do it, *when, where,* and *why.* To perform a skill or develop a competence, we have to create *an internal documentary Film*. Such a film gives us a prototype for how to succeed in accomplishing our outcomes.

Take a moment to consider some of the skills and behaviors that you have learned to do. What areas of expertise are you competent and skilled at? Riding a bike, skating, cooking a meal, waiting on customers, answering the phone, working on a computer, selling, etc.?

As you just "think" about the activity, notice the Movie that you activate from your video archives. This is your documentary film about *how to do it*. To say that we know *how* to do something is to say, "Yes I have a film in my mind-body system for that one."

When Neo in *The Matrix* saw a helicopter on top of the building that housed the Agent's headquarters, he pointed to it and asked Trinity, "Do you know how to fly that?" She said, "Not yet." Then she dialed their 'operator' Tank and asked him for the program. As he accessed the file of the educational video for flying that particular helicopter, her eyes fluttered for a few moments. She then said, "Let's go." Talk about accelerated learning!

Competence in any skill involves seeing, hearing, and feeling all of the various facets and features of *a set of behaviors* along with the necessary theoretical knowledge. When we first learn, we often ask to see a procedure again and again, sometimes multiple times, until we get it. We learn a script, a way of talking, the jargon of the field. We practice. We get our hands on the instruments, the tools, and we may receive personal mentoring by an older and more experienced practitioner.

In the mind, our video films of how-to information move up the levels until they become our *frame of reference and frame of mind*. We then know it so well we don't even have to think about it. We know it without thinking, we know it intuitively. In fact, thinking about it might mess up our "intuitive" feel of it. At this level, the competence is just a "feeling." We know it in our muscles. This is true of motor skill activities like tennis, baseball, working on an assembly line. It is also true for learning a part in a play, playing an instrument, doing surgery, and so on. When it reaches this level, we have become unconsciously competent.

At the level of unconscious competence we typically *cannot* explain the expertise. If we wanted to teach or mentor someone in the skill, we would have to tolerate the jarring and tongue-tying feeling that occurs when we try to do and show and talk about what has dropped beneath conscious awareness. This is the price we pay in our mind-body system in order to bring it back into consciousness. After we do that for awhile, we can then move to a yet higher level and become conscious enough of our unconscious competence to talk about it.

Generating New Skill Sets and Behaviors
We can now apply "skills as a documentary film" as a template for learning any other skill. In fact, thinking about it as a Movie documentary and moving around it from multiple perspectives, so that we can see and experience it from various positions as well as from the editor's and director's point of view, gives us a way to accelerate our competence.

Competence Accelerator Pattern:
1) Name your Movie.

> What skill, behaviors, or competence would you like to develop?
>
> Who do you know that can already do this at an expert

level?

2) Create a well-formed outcome.

Make a vivid and accurate film of your desired outcome in learning this new skill or competency. Produce an internal Movie of this skill so that you have a clear, vivid, and specific description of what you want.

What do you want?

What resources do you need to make this become a reality?

What does the skill look like, sound like, feel like?

3) Step into the film of the competency.

When you have a Cinema in your mind of the behaviors, step into the Movie and let it play out in your mind.

When you step into the Movie, what does it look like, sound like, and feel like from within?

What are the steps and stages in the process?

4) Step out and edit the Movie with what you're learning.

Whenever you learn even the tiniest distinction that helps to refine and improve the Movie, step out, edit it in.

What does the film now look like as you observe it from outside?

What words, ideas, understandings are you editing into the Movie that makes it richer and fuller?

Do you now have the strategy for the set of skills?

What else do you need?

5) Step in and test.

As you step back in with these new distinctions, how does it now feel?

6) Keep using your sensory awareness to calibrate and track your progress.

Is the film now a good map for this skill?

What feedback are you discovering from inside, outside, and the other positions?

As you step into the director and producer perspectives, what other feedback are you receiving that you can use to refine the film even further?

7) Receive the feedback and compare it to your original goal.

Given the feedback, what do you now need to do?

What adjustments or variations do you need to make?

Are you moving in the right direction?

Do you need other resources to assist you?

Can you now get the results that you want?

Are you progressing step-by-step along the way?

What lets you know?

8) Keep repeating this process.

If you are moving in the right direction, how much persistence do you need?

What do you need to keep up your motivation?

Are you acknowledging and validating your progress?

Components for Producing a Top-Notch Training Film

There are certain elements that we need to incorporate in any *training film* that we will use to develop new skills. These utilize our full neuro-linguistic and neuro-semantic system for creating an internal Cinema using all of the cinematic positions and levels. As an overview, we need to have full use of the following components.

1) Clean sensory awareness.

Sensory acuity is what allows us to cleanly see and hear and feel as well as to calibrate to what's actually happening. This means getting out of our abstract levels of mind and "coming to our senses." When we do that then we can cleanly track from good models and mentors to our mental Movie. It's difficult, if not impossible, to film *how to do* something if we do not have clean sense receptors. In learning new skills that's why we often have to see and then re-see to detect all of the necessary distinctions.

2) Awareness of cinematic features.

Our increased awareness of the particular cinematic features in our Movies, and of other possibilities, gives us the ability to more fully use our senses. We begin by discerning our internal default settings and then developing the flexibility to shift and alter these settings in our internal Movie.

An excellent speller, for example, has to be able to make internal images, to hold them, and to manipulate them. Over the years, we have found that by making the letters bigger, brighter, or to alter their shape (bright red block shape letters), facilitates the skill.

3) Editorial skills.

Practicing and assuming our full editorial prerogatives for what we can do inside as we make the cinema more compelling, vivid, exciting, and vital is also a part of this art. We need the ability to effectively use our cinematic video and sound tracks to give clear instructions to ourselves when we play the actor's role. In fact, stepping in and out of our film gives us the ability to keep editing it until it is just right.

4) Jumping logical levels.

Another crucial element is the ability to detect and direct the higher levels of our mind. To move to the director and executive levels where we set our highest intentions, designs, motivations, and purposes. When we rise up to the executive levels of mind, then we become the producers of our own internal Movies. Then we can make sure that we direct and edit our Cinema Mind in just the right way, with just the right qualities and properties. For many skills we need the right motivation and sufficiently strong enough motivation to do it at the expert level. This means setting a big enough *why* (or reason) for the skill. This is obvious for those who climb Mount Everest. It is also true for the skills involved in building wealth in a decade.

5) *Quality control checks.*

In jumping logical levels, we need the ability the move to a place where we can step back and check the quality of life, behaviors, relationships, feelings, etc. within our entire mind-body system. This skill enables us to create Movies that will keep us balanced and whole. It allows us to make our productions rewarding ones.

6) *Flexibility and adaptability.*

Crucial in all of this is the openness and flexibility to detect and receive feedback as information and to then use such in editing and refining new features into our Movies.

7) *Resilience.*

For continual improvement, we need the persistence to stay with a skill and to keep coming back, "bouncing back" when we get knocked down. This allows us to keep learning so that we can master a given area.

Tossing Out the "Failure" Film

If these components are necessary to produce and use in any good training film that instructs us in how to become more skilled, masterful, and successful, then any current Movie of "Failure and Defeat" that we may default to when things don't go our way will undermine our learning.

Do you have any *Failure Flicks* that play in the theater of your mind? "Failure," of course, is one of those nominalizations (actions turned into a noun) that gives the impression that one action, or a series of actions, that didn't immediately succeed somehow dooms or fates us to "never succeed." Linguistically it freezes the action so that it sounds like a thing. It is not. It is merely a frame of mind about non-successful events.

As a nominalization, the term "failure" means that we have generalized this higher frame of mind or attitude from some events to create this classification. This records a *Failure Film* and leaves us with that as our meta-feeling or perspective about things. Do this often enough and it becomes easy to use this film as your identity frame and to see all of life through this filter. Hence the screen play, "I am a failure." "My whole life has been a failure and that means my whole future will be nothing more than a failure."

To this low quality film, let's ask some indexing questions to un-glue the psycho-logics encoded within.

> *What* did you fail at?
> *When* did you fail at this?
> *What criteria* and standards do you use in making this evaluation?
> *How often* did you fail at it?
> What have you learned that will help you to succeed from

now on?

What adjustments do you plan to make?

Does anything stop you from continuing and using your knowledge?

These indexing questions enable us to make a copy of the internal Movie that torments this person so that we can understand how he or she does it, and at the same time, the questions invite the person to transform the film. Like a ruthless movie critic, these questions call the screenplay, acting, meaning, purpose, quality, etc. of the Movie into question. They invite the actor to re-read the lines with some critical thinking skills to see if the plot of the Movie really makes any sense.

The origin of such sick documentaries were made innocently enough. We simply filmed non-success experiences and then, as director, decided that this means "failure" and so we began producing a serious, dangerous, and predictive Movie of the future *"The Dangers of Failing in Life."*

But enough of that. It doesn't enhance life. It does not empower us to learn and to take more informed risks. It's a B-rated film that we no longer need to play in the theater of our mind. It's ready for the trash heap, is it not?

Summary

- The Movies that play on the screen in our mind determine what we can do, the actions possible in our repertoire of behaviors, and our skill level. We can only play the roles that we have a Movie for.
- Recognizing that skills of competence arise from the educational films that we've learned and developed gives us yet another way to use our CinemaMind more effectively.

Chapter 13

THE NEURO-SEMANTICS
OF OUR CINEMA MIND

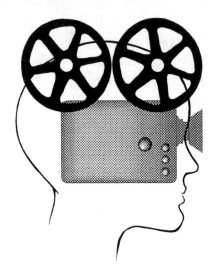

Having presented a *cinematic model of mind* based upon two principal models, NLP and Neuro-Semantics, it's now time to talk about these models and give you the straight story. These cutting edge models describe the mind-body-emotion system from the standpoint of structure and experience. That is, how we *experience* mind and our experiences. From that we can learn the structure of the experience.

Given that we have taken a *metaphor* about how we function and experience things and we have run with it through this entire work, it seems appropriate for those who want to know more about the source and foundation of this work that we now describe NLP and Neuro-Semantics. That's the purpose of this final chapter.

Both NLP and NS excel for describing mind in terms of a Cinema. That is, it is very easy to translate the more technical cognitive-behavioral terms of representation modalities and systems (i.e., the visual, auditory, kinesthetic) in terms of an internal Movie. The reason I've done this is to make these cutting edge cognitive-behavioral models more available. I want to make them more user-friendly. Having done that, this last chapter presents the source models themselves.

NLP: Neuro-Linguistic Programming
At its heart, NLP is a model of communication. It arose from a transformational grammar professor (John Grinder) and a student of mathematics, computers, and gestalt therapy (Richard Bandler). They built the model after they encountered three world-class therapists (Virginia Satir, Fritz Perls, and Milton Erickson) and saw "the magic" they could perform via advanced communication skills. So NLP is fundamentally about how we process information as we send signals to our brain-and-body that format our experiences. In this way NLP is about "running our own brain" and managing our states.

NLP uses the "languages" of mind (i.e., the visual, auditory, and kinesthetic modalities) which we have here described as our internal Cinema of sights, sounds, and sensations. It also uses the meta-representation system of language which we have here translated to the sound track and the screenplay of our mental theater. Recognizing that we "think" and frame things using these *see, hear, and feel* dimensions, we have the leverages for controlling what goes on upstairs.

NLP works with our mind-body states at both the neurological level and the linguistic level to identify our "programs" that run the show. As a model of human functioning, NLP primarily utilized two metaphors, the map metaphor and the computer programming metaphor.

"The map is not the territory" was the original premise of Alfred Korzybski who wrote *Science and Sanity* (1933) and initiated studies in neuro-linguistics. He originated that phrase to indicate that mind-body work together as a single system. *Mapping* is probably the most common metaphor in NLP about human thinking-and-feeling. From that Bandler and Grinder picked up on the mapping or modeling processes as they identified that when we construct a map or facsimile of something we leave things out (deletion), we summarize (generalization) and we alter things (distortion). The map metaphor also predominates NLP in terms of modeling experts and the strategies of genius.

The next most dominate metaphor in NLP is *the computer metaphor.* This makes perfect sense given the studies of Bandler in the computer sciences and the dominance of that metaphor in the field of the cognitive sciences. It was this metaphor that led to the unfortunate term in the name, "programming." While this made perfect sense in the context of the brain-body as the hardware and the mind as *the software* having many "programs" for how to operate, it carries with it other connotations. As a metaphor it contained entailments of control, manipulation, brain washing, etc. Many people around the world have actually changed the "P" of NLP to psychology, psychotherapy, processing, etc. to get away from the idea of programming which sounded too much like control.

The focus of NLP has always been very practical rather than

abstract or academic. The model has focused on what works, and how it works, and has consciously avoided theory, theory-construction, and philosophy. This has been its strength and its weakness.

Neuro-Semantics

Neuro-Semantics arose from the foundation of NLP and extends it to include the higher or meta-levels. The term refers to the fact that we create *meanings* in our minds (semantics) and become those meanings incorporated in our bodies (neurology). This is why, when things *mean* something to us—we *feel* it in our bodies. The meanings show up in what we call "emotions." The meanings take the form of values, ideas, beliefs, understandings, paradigms, mental models, frames, etc.

Neuro-Semantics describes how we make meaning as we evaluate experiences, events, words, etc. and how we then live in the world of meaning that we construct or inherit. As a model, it describes the frames of reference we use as we move through life and the frames of meaning that we construct. It allows us to specify the matrix of Frames in which we live, and from which, we operate.

Neuro-Semantics emerged from the *Meta-States model*. Meta-states describes the levels of states or mind that we experience. That's because we never just think. As soon as we think or feel—we then experience thoughts and feelings *about* the first thought, then other thoughts-and-feelings about that thought, and so on. Technically this is called "self-reflective consciousness."

A model of reflexive consciousness, Meta-States extends NLP. It details precisely how we *reflect back on* our thoughts and feelings to create *higher levels* of thoughts-and-feelings and layers of consciousness. In so using our thoughts-and-feelings thoughts-

about-our-thoughts, feelings-*about*-feelings, we create mind-body *states-about-states* or meta-states.

The NLP Metaphor of Mental Movies

While NLP has mostly used the "map" and the computer "programming" metaphors, from the beginning Bandler and Grinder did sometimes use, or imply, *the movie metaphor.* In fact, Bandler especially began using the movie metaphor when he explored what he called "sub-modalities." He used this term for the cinematic features of our Movies. In his book *Using Your Brain—For a Change* (1985), he used the movie metaphor frequently as a way to talk about "running your own brain."

Yet there was a flaw in the term "sub-modalities." Mostly, the name was wrong. The name was not just mildly wrong, it was significantly wrong. It misdirected us about the cinematic features, how to understand them, and how to use them effectively. The prefix "sub" implies that these features or elements of the modalities were somehow *under* or *lower* than the representational systems of our Movies. The error began with this misunderstanding. As we have seen, cinematic features are *the frames* that we use for our Movies, the editorial films. That puts them at a higher logical level, not a lower one.

Actually, Todd Epstein was the first to name these cinematic features in NLP. He originally called them ***pragmagraphics.*** As the *graphic* features of the Movies that have *pragmatic effects* on our states—that would have been a much better label than "sub-modalities." If you're interested in that, we have an entire book on this subject, see *The Structure of Excellence: Unmasking the Meta-Levels of "Sub-Modalities"* (1999).

Four Meta-Domains

In NLP and NS, there are four meta-domains. These four models give us four ways of describing experience and hence four redundant avenues for structurally formatting an experience. We used these in this work although we did not make them explicit. Now for the explicit version. The four domains that are all *meta* to our representations at the primary level are these:

> *1) The domain of language*—described and formulated by the Meta-Model.
>
> *2) The domain of the cinematic features of our representation systems*— described and formulated by the "Sub-Modalities" model.

Figure 13:1

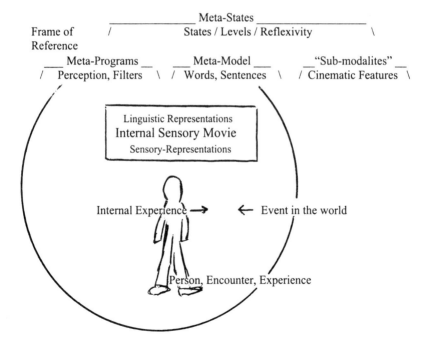

3) The domain of the perceptual filters by which we sort for and pay attention to things—described and formulated by the Meta-Programs.

4) The domain of logical levels and reflexivity that creates states upon states —described and formulated by the Meta-States model.

In this work, we have described representation modalities and systems as *the Movie* playing in the theater of our mind. Above that we have the *Editorial* position where we edit in the cinematic features (the "sub-modalities" or more accurately, the meta-modalities). Above that we have the *director's* position that uses the screen play (language, the Meta-Model) for determining the cinematic features and for giving guidance to the structure of the Movie. At that level and above we have the *Producer and Executive levels* that correspond to the states and attitudes (Meta-States) and perceptions and focus of the Movie (Meta-Programs).

NLP/NS and Developmental Psychology
So, which comes first? Language, perception, Movies with cinematic distinctions, or state?

Since we are not born with language, but learn language, an infant does not yet *linguistically map* the territory. Instead, the infant immediately *senses* the world at the primary level. "Thought" for the infant is mere *representation*. And even that is very primitive. As infants we are not born with the ability to hold our images constant. What we see, hear, feel, smell, and taste on the outside comes and goes. When mother leaves the room, she's gone and we can't see her in our mind. Constancy of representation will come later. In the meantime we holler and scream because we cannot comfort ourselves with an internal image of mother. And, we giggle and laugh when she plays peek-a-boo with us, constantly giving us a cognitive jar as she keeps reappearing out of nowhere.

But with "constancy of representation," mental and emotional life takes on an entirely new dimension. We can now "record" our Movies of what we see, hear, feel, etc. and keep those Movies in our mind to entertain us. Now we can "think" by playing the Movies over and over and take them wherever we go. Yet it isn't long before we reach yet another developmental stage, soon we can have "second thoughts" while experiencing the first thoughts. That is, *while* we are playing a Movie of playing, eating, resting, watching TV, etc., we can have yet another thought *about* that.

At a training, a participant said that his eight-month old little girl had become so constipated that "going to the potty" had become painful. With this she became afraid of going to the toilet. Yet he had found a solution. He went with her and sang to her while she sat on the potty. The singing would distract her mind and she could go. But when he learned about the art of anchoring, he asked,

> Would this anchor of music in the bathroom to trigger the "going to potty" response set up any undesirable consequences in the future?

An interesting question, and one that evoked a lot of laughter about the possibilities. Yet even more fascinating to me was the child's meta-state. Even at that early age she could already *anticipate* with *fear* going to the toilet. She had already enough reflexivity in her little mind to not only anticipate and hold constant the idea and experience of going to the potty, and it being unpleasant, but had come to *fear* that unpleasantness.

The state of pain was one thing, her *fear of* anticipating that pain was yet another. It was a higher frame of mind (a meta-state) about her Movie. She was already setting a frame of fear at the editorial and director levels about her experiences or Movies. Once we become reflexive, our self-reflexive consciousness and use of language to track and anchor such states becomes our way of perceiving the world or the dominate Movie for making sense of life.

This introduction to NLP has been to make it more user-friendly. If you're interested in more about the fabulous and magical world of NLP and Neuro-Semantics, see the section of books at the end of this book.

Summary

- In this book I have run with the *Movie metaphor* to provide a user-friendly version of NLP and Neuro-Semantics. These are models about the structure of experience, models that assume that if we can identify the structure, we can replicate it.
- These models are also about how to practically "run our own brain" so that we can take charge of our mind, emotions, and states.

PRINCIPLES
OF MENTAL CINEMATOGRAPHY

1) To "think" is to entertain a mental snapshot or movie of sights, sounds, sensations, etc. on the theater of our mind.

2) Because our mental Movies create our states, the cinemas in our video-library are not neutral. They affect our body, mind, health, sanity, and resourcefulness

3) There's a critical difference between *experiencing* our mental Movies and *being consciously aware* of our Movies. One is about consciousness, the other about consciousness of consciousness.

4) The pictures that flash through our mind-body-emotion system zoom through in nanoseconds. The ability to hold them still, observe them, and manipulate them is a developed skill that comes with practice.

5) If we don't take charge of our mental Movies, someone else will simply supply us with them and run the Movies they want in our minds.

6) The idea of having mental Movies in our heads is just a metaphor, yet a useful and productive one for self-understanding and self-control. There's no real or literal screen in our mind, it just seems that there is.

7) We "think" and "make sense" of things by creating mental Movies that film, record, store, and use these Movies as maps for navigating through life. We "understand" something to the extent that we can track it over onto the screen of our mind.

8) When we change key cinematic features in our Movies—we not only change the Movie, but our internal world and with it our actions, speech, behaviors, skills, and feelings.

9) The Movies playing in the theater of our mind create our emotions. Behind every emotion is a Movie.

10) It takes a hierarchy to create a Movie and so there are levels of Movie production in the mind, from the level of playing the actor, to editing, directing,

and producing.

11) The levels of the mind give us the ability to take many perceptual positions on things. Doing so enriches and enhances our understandings, gives us more perspective, and so allows greater wisdom to emerge.

SPECIALIZED VOCABULARY

Meta: "Meta" refers to something above and beyond something else, it refers to something at a higher level. At that level it is *about* the lower. We transcend the lower, including it in the higher classification and so create meta or logical levels.

Meta-States: States *about* states, thoughts about thoughts, feelings about feelings, the second thoughts-emotions that we entertain about the first ones, the ways we react to our own reactions.

Nominalization:

When *naming* (nominalize) a verb or set of actions, we turn the verb into a false-noun because it really does *not* stand for a "person, place, or thing," nothing real and tangible. It stands for an idea or set of actions that have been frozen and hidden in what seems like an entity. This reifies the actions. In this way, *relating* is frozen and hidden in relationship. *Moving* and *motive* is hidden in motivation. *Depressing, guilting, angering, langauging,* etc. is hidden in depression, guilt, anger, language.

Neuro-Linguistic Programming:

A communication model regarding how we think and process information using our minds (linguistics) and bodies (neurology) to create our "programs" for operating in the world. A model of human functioning that focuses on the structure of experience so that we can "run our own brains."

Neuro-Semantics:

A model about how we use our nervous systems and brain (neurology) to create and encode meaning (semantics) in our body. A cognitive model of human functioning based upon *NLP* and *Meta-States* that describes self-reflexive consciousness.

Representation Systems:

We represent information using the sensory systems and so "think" by seeing, hearing, feeling, using language, etc.

Bibliography

Bandler, Richard; and Grinder, John. (1975, 1976). *The structure of magic, Volumes I & II: A book about language and therapy.* Palo Alto, CA: Science & Behavior Books.

Bandler, Richard; and Grinder, John. (1979). *Frogs into princes: Neuro-linguistic programming.* Moab, UT: Real People Press.

Bandler, Richard. (1985). *Using your brain for a change: Neuro-linguistic programming.* Moab, UT: Real People Press.

Bandler, Richard; Will McDonald. (1988). *An insider's guide to submodalities.* Capitola, CA: Meta Publications.

Bateson, Gregory. (1972/2000). *Steps to an ecology of mind.* Chicago, IL: University of Chicago.

Bateson, Gregory. (1979). *Mind and nature: A necessary unity.* New York: Bantam.

Bodenhamer, Bobby G.; and Hall, L. Michael (1997). *Time-lining: Advanced patterns in "Time" Processes.* Wales, UK: Anglo-American Books.

Bodenhamer, Bobby G.; Hall, L. Michael. (1999). *The user's manual for the brain: A comprehensive manual for neuro-linguistic programming practitioner certification.* United Kingdom: Crown House Publishers.

Capra, Fritjof. (1996). *The web of life.* New York: Anchor/ Doubleday.

Dilts, R.B. (1990). *Changing beliefs systems with NLP.* Cupertino, CA: Meta Publications.

Dilts, R.B.; Dilts, R.W.; Epstein, Todd. (1991). *Tools for dreamers: Strategies for creativity and the structure of innovation.* Cupertino, CA: Meta Publications.

Dilts, Robert B. (1994). *Strategies of Genius, Volume I. Aristotle, Sherlock Homes, Walt Disney, Wolfgang Amadeus Mozart.* Capitola, CA: Meta Publications.

Dilts, Robert B. (1994). *Strategies of Genius, Volume II. Einstein.* Capitola, CA: Meta Publications.

Dilts, Robert B. (1995). *Strategies of Genius, Volume III. Freud, Mozart.* Capitola, CA: Meta Publications.

Gardner, Howard. (198X). *Frames of mind: The theory of multiple intelligences.* NY: BasicBooks.

Gardner, Howard. (1991). *The unschooled mind: How children think and how schools should teach.* NY: HarperCollins.

Gardner, Howard. (1993). *Multiple intelligences: The theory in practice.* NY: BasicBooks.

Goleman, Daniel. (1995). *Emotional intelligence.* New York: Bantam books.

Hall, L. Michael. (1995/2000). *Meta-states: Mastering the higher levels of the mind.* Grand Junction, CO: Neuro-Semantic Publications.

Hall, L. Michael. (2001). *Communication magic.* Formerly, *The secrets of magic* (1998). Wales, UK: Anglo-American Books.

Hall, Michael. (1996/2000 2nd ed.). *The spirit of NLP: Mastering the art.* Wales, UK: Anglo-American Books.

Hall, L. Michael. (2000). *Dragon slaying: Dragons to princes.* Grand Jct., CO: ET Publications. (2nd edition).

Hall, Michael L. (1996). *Becoming a ferocious presenter.* Grand Jct., CO: ET Publications.

Hall, Michael L. (1996d). *Languaging: The linguistics of psychotherapy.* Grand Jct., CO: ET Publications.

Hall, Michael; Bodenhamer, Bob. (1997). *Mind-lines: Lines for changing minds.* Grand Jct., CO: Neuro-Semantic Publications.

Hall, Michael; Bodenhamer, Bob. (1999). *The Structure of excellence: Unmasking the meta-levels of "sub-modalities."* Grand Jct. CO., ET

Publications.

Hall, L. Michael; Bodenhamer, Bob. (1997). *Figuring out people: Design engineering using meta-programs.* Wales, UK: Anglo-American Books.

Hall, L. Michael; Belnap, Barbara. (1997). *The sourcebook of magic.* Wales, UK: Crown House Publications.

Hall, L. Michael. (2000). *Frame Games: Persuasion elegance.* Grand Jct., CO: Neuro-Semantics Publications.

Hall. L. Michael. (2000). *Secrets of personal mastery.* Wales, UK: Crown House Publications.

Hall, L. Michael. (2002). *The Matrix Model.* Clifton, CO: Neuro-Semantic Publication.

Hatcher, Jeffrey. (1996). *The art and craft of playwriting.* Cincinnati, OH. Story Press F. & W. Publishers.

Korzybski, Alfred. (1933/ 1994). *Science and sanity: An introduction to non-Aristotelian systems and general semantics.* (5th. ed.). Lakeville, CN: International Non-Aristotelian Library Publishing Co.

Maslow, Abraham. (1950). *Motivation and personality.*

O'Connor, Joseph; and Seymour, John. (1990). *Introducing neuro-linguistic programming: The new psychology of personal excellence.* Bodmin, Cornwall, UK: Hartnolls Limited.

Pert, Candice B. (1997). *Molecules of emotion: Why you feel the way you feel.* New York: Scribner.

Robbins, Anthony. (1989). *Unlimited power: The new science of personal achievement.* NY: Simon and Schuster.

THE AUTHOR

L. Michael Hall, Ph.D.
P.O. Box 8
Clifton, Colorado, 81520 USA
(970) 523-7877
Michael@neurosemantics.com
www.runyourownbrain.com

Dr. L. Michael Hall earned his doctorate in Cognitive-Behavioral Psychology with a special emphasis in psycho-linguistics. He has long been interested in the structure of "mind" and developing practical models and tools for providing more freedom, mastery, and power in taking charge of our own minds. His dissertation dealt with the *languaging* of four psychotherapies (NLP, RET, Reality Therapy, Logotherapy) using the formulations of General Semantics.

After many years as a psychotherapist in private practice, Dr. Hall began running trainings in assertiveness, negotiations, conflict management, anger control, and then NLP. After studying with Richard Bandler in the late 1980s, he began modeling and developed *the Meta-States Model* (1994) while modeling *resilience.*

As a prolific writer, Michael has written over 30 books including *The Spirit of NLP*, *Becoming a more Ferocious Presenter, Dragon Slaying, Meta-States, Mind-Lines, Figuring Out People, The Structure of Excellence, Frame Games,* etc.

Today as a psychologist and entrepreneur, Dr. Hall lives in the Colorado Rocky Mountains where he writes, travels internationally on behalf of the *The International Society of Neuro-Semantics* and continues to create new models.

Books:

> *Meta-States: Managing the higher states of your mind (2000)*
> *Dragon Slaying: Dragons to Princes (2000, 2nd edition)*
> *The Spirit of NLP: The Process, Meaning & Criteria for*

Mastering NLP (1996)

Languaging: The Linguistics of Psychotherapy (1996)

Patterns For "Renewing the Mind" (w. Dr. Bodenhamer) (1997)

Time-Lining: Advance Time-Line Processes (w. Dr. Bodenhamer) (1997)

NLP: Going Meta—Advanced Modeling Using Meta-Levels (2001)

Figuring Out People: Design Engineering With Meta-Programs (w. Dr. Bodenhamer) (1997)

A Sourcebook of Magic (formerly, How to Do What When (w. B. Belnap) (1999)

Mind Lines: Lines For Changing Minds (w. Dr. Bodenhamer) (1997, 2002).

Communicational Magic for the 21ˢᵗ. Century (2001).

Meta-States Magic: formerly the MS *Journal* (97, 98, 99)

The Structure of Excellence: Unmasking the Meta-Levels of Submodalities (Hall and Bodenhamer, 1999)

Instant Relaxation (1999, Lederer & Hall)

The User's Manual of the Brain (1999, w. Bodenhamer)

Secrets of Personal Mastery (2000)

Frame Games: Persuasion Elegance (2000)

The Structure of Personality: Modeling "Personality" Using NLP and Neuro-Semantics. (Hall , Bodenhamer, Bolstad, Harmblett, 2001)

Games Slim People Play (2001)

Games Business Experts Play (2002)

The Matrix Model (2002)

The User's Manual of the Brain, Volume II (2003, w. Bodenhamer).

TRAININGS AVAILABLE

NLP TRAININGS:

Meta-NLP Practitioner:

An intensive 7-day training in the Essential NLP Skills. This training introduces NLP as a model for discovering the structure of human functioning with a focus on *how to run your own brain* and to manage your own states. Learn the basic rapport-building, listening, and influence skills of NLP, as well as how to access and manage states through anchoring, reframing, and using dozens of NLP patterns. Discover how to use language both for precision and hypnotic influence. Required reading, *User's Manual for the Brain* and *The Sourcebook of Magic.*

Meta-Masters NLP Practitioner:

An intensive 13-Day Training in mastering all three of the meta-domains of NLP: Language (Meta-Model), Perception (Meta-Programs) and States and Levels (Meta-States). This training focuses on the pathway to mastery and how to develop the very spirit of NLP—curiosity, accelerated learning, flexibility, confidence, passion, playfulness, etc.

Basic Meta-State Trainings

Accessing Personal Genius (The 3 day Basic).

Introduction to Meta-States as an advanced NLP model (3 days). This training introduces and teaches the *Meta-States Model* and is ideal for NLP Practitioners. It presupposes knowledge of the NLP Model and builds the training around accessing the kinds of states that will access and support "personal genius."

Basic Meta-States in two other Simplified forms:

1) Secrets of Personal Mastery: Awakening Your Inner Executive.

This training presents the power of Meta-States *without* directly teaching the model as such. The focus instead shifts to *Personal Mastery* and the *Executive Powers* of the participants. Formatted so that it can take the form of 1, 2 or 3 days, this training presents a simpler form of Meta-States, especially good for those without NLP background or those who are more focused on Meta-States Applications than the model.

2) Frame Games: Persuasion Elegance.

The first truly *User Friendly* version of Meta-States. Frame Games provides practice and use of Meta-States in terms of frame detecting, setting, and changing. As a model of frames, Frame Games focuses on the power of persuasion via frames and so presents how to influence or persuade yourself and others using the Levels of Thought or Mind that lies at the heart of Meta-States. Designed as a 3 day program, the first two days presents the model of Frame Games and lots of exercises. Day three is for becoming a true Frame Game Master and working with frames conversationally and covertly.

Meta-States Gateway Trainings

1) Wealth Building (Meta-Wealth).

The focus of this training is on learning how to think like a millionaire, to develop the mind and meta-mind of someone who is structured and programmed to create wealth economically, personally, mentally, emotionally, relationally, etc. As a Meta-States Application Training, Wealth Building Excellence began as a modeling project and seeks to facilitate the replication of that excellence in participants.

2) Games Great Sales People Play (Meta-Selling).

Another Meta-States Application Training, modeled after experts in the fields of selling and persuasion and designed to replicate in participants. An excellent follow-up training to Wealth Building since most people who build wealth have to sell their ideas and dreams to others. This trainings goes way beyond mere Persuasion Engineering as it uses the Strategic Selling model of Heiman also known as Relational Selling, Facilitation Selling, etc.

3) Mind-Lines: Lines for Changing Minds.

Based upon the book by Drs. Hall and Bodenhamer (1997), now in its third edition, Mind-Line Training is a training about Conversational Reframing and Persuasion. The Mind-Lines model began as a rigorous update of the old NLP "Sleight of Mouth" Patterns and has grown to become the persuasion language of the Meta-State moves. This advanced training is highly and mainly a linguistic model, excellent as a follow-up training for Wealth Building and Selling Excellence. Generally a two day format, although sometimes 3 and 4 days.

4) Accelerated Learning Using NLP & Meta-States (Meta-Learning).

A Meta-State Application training based upon the NLP model for "running your own brain" and the Neuro-Semantic (Meta-States) model of managing your higher executive states of consciousness. Modeled after leading experts in the fields of education, cognitive psychologies, this training provides extensive insight into the Learning States and how to access your personal learning genius. It provides specific strategies for various learning tasks as well as processes for research and writing.

5) Defusing Hotheads:

A Meta-States and NLP Application training for handling hot, stressed-out, and irrational people in Fight/Flight states. Designed to "talk someone down from a hot angry state," this training provides training in state management, first for the skilled negotiator or manager, and then for eliciting another into a more resourceful state. Based upon the book by Dr. Hall, *Defusing Strategies (1987),* this training has been presented to managers and supervisors for greater skill in conflict management, and to police departments for coping with domestic violence.

6) Instant Relaxation.

A practical NLP and Meta-States Application Training designed to facilitate the advanced ability to quickly "fly into a calm." Based in part upon the book by Lederer and Hall (Instant Relaxation, 1999), this training does not teach NLP or Meta-States, but coaches the relaxation skills for greater "presence of mind," control over mind and neurology, and empowerment in handling stressful situations. An excellent training in conjunction with Defusing Hotheads.

7) Games for Mastering Fear.

To play the Game of Fear, a person has to run his or her brain in a certain way using special frames. The same is true for mastering fear—the power of transformation lies in knowing how to identify the right frames and set them at the higher levels of our mind. This training uses the very best of NLP and Neuro-Semantic patterns to provide true mastery over any kind of fear that might sabotage or limit living up to our Visions and Values. Based upon the book by this title by Hall and Bodenhamer.

8) Games For Mastering Stuttering (Blocking).

There's a structure to the meta-state experience called "stuttering," it is blocking our non-fluency and layering it with a painful kind of self-consciousness. There's also a structure to mastering that experience and moving toward a less semantically over-loading. This training is based on NLP and Neuro-Semantic patterns and structured according to the 7 Mind Matrix model.

9) Games Business Experts Play.

Succeeding in business necessitates develop a certain expertise and business wisdom about oneself, others, skills, markets, finances, managing, etc. Those who do it best, the experts, have a strategy and a certain set of frames of mind that allow them to play those Games. Based upon the book by this title, this training invites you to set the kind of frames of mind and meaning that will bring out your business expertise.

10) Games Slim and Fit People Play.

How do they do it? How do some people relate to eating and exercising in such a way that it is "no problem" to them? What are the frames and games that slim and fit people play so that food does *not* dominate their lives and so that they have plenty of energy and vitality? That's the focus of this training, based on the book by the same title. The training offers specific guidance about how to stop psycho-eating and to develop a much better relationship to both food and movement.

Advanced Neuro-Semantic Trainings
Advanced Modeling Using Meta-Levels:

Advanced use of Meta-States by focusing on the domain of modeling excellence. This training typically occurs as the last 4 days of the 7 day Meta-States Certification. Based upon the modeling experiences of Dr. Hall and his book, *NLP: Going Meta— Advanced Modeling Using Meta-Levels,* this training looks at the formatting and structuring of the meta-levels in Resilience, Un-Insultability, and Seeing Opportunities. The training touches on modeling of Wealth Building, Fitness, Women in Leadership, Persuasion, etc.

Advanced Flexibility Training

An advanced Neuro-Semantics training that explores the riches and treasures in Alfred Korzybski's work, *Science and Sanity.* Originally presented in London (1998, 1999) as "The Merging of the Models: NLP and General Semantics," this training now focuses almost exclusively on *developing Advanced Flexibility* using tools, patterns, and models in General Semantics. Recommend for the advanced student of NLP and Meta States.

Neuro-Semantics and NLP Trainers Training.

An advanced training for those who have been certified in Meta-States and Neuro-Semantics (the seven day program). This application training focuses the power and magic of Meta-States on the training experience itself—both public and individual training. It focuses first on the trainer, to access one's own Top Training States and then on how to meta-states or set the frames when working with others in coaching or facilitating greater resourcefulness.

Neuro-Semantics Coaching Certification Training.

An advanced 7 day Training for those with Meta-NLP training and preferably *Personal Genius.* Based on the 7 Matrices Model that arose from *Frame Games* which arose from *Meta-States*, this model ties all of the patterns in NLP and Neuro-Semantics together into a package that allows a person to coach and/or do therapy with these patterns.